READING THE OLD TESTAMENT PROPHETS TODAY

Harry Mowvley

John Knox Press
ATLANTA

A special edition published by arrangement with
Lutterworth Press, London, England
© Copyright Harry Mowvley 1979

Library of Congress Cataloging in Publication Data

Mowvley, Harry.
　　Reading the Old Testament prophets today.

　　Includes bibliographical references and indexes.
　　　1. Prophets. 2. Bible. O.T. Prophets—
Criticism, interpretation, etc. I. Title.
BS1198.M68　　　224'.06　　　79-87744
ISBN 0-8042-0167-6

Printed in the United States of America
John Knox Press
Atlanta, Georgia 1979

READING THE OLD TESTAMENT PROPHETS TODAY

Contents

I

Prophetic Call
and Inspiration

1. Prophecy in Israel and the Ancient Near East

The word 'prophecy' has come to mean 'the power of telling what will happen in the future'.[1] Consequently the prophets of the Old Testament are commonly understood as men who fulfil this function and their writings have been searched for predictions both of the life and death of Jesus Christ and of events due to take place at the end of time which from our point of view are still in the future. The definition is not entirely inaccurate when it is applied to the Old Testament prophets but it is misleading in two respects.

First it would be a serious limitation of their work to imagine that they were only concerned with future events. Any serious reading of the prophetic books reveals a concern with contemporary affairs upon which they comment often in the strongest possible terms. So it is frequently said that the 'pro-' in prophecy signifies not fore-telling but forth-telling.[2] They tell forth the message of God to the people of their own day concerning circumstances of their own day. Second, this sometimes involved predictions about the future based upon observation of the present and when this was so they were not slow to say what they believed was about to happen. But generally this future was near at hand. It concerned the coming fate of the people to whom they spoke and not events that should happen thousands of years hence. Destruction, defeat in battle, the fall of Jerusalem, the exile in Babylon were all future events of which the prophets spoke in advance before they happened, but they were to happen soon.

Yet besides this, they did sometimes look further into the future beyond the coming disaster and their faith in God enabled them to express hopes which were by no means immediately fulfilled. This is not to say, as some have done, that the prophets were speaking directly of the coming of

Christ or of the end of the world. Nothing was so definite in their minds. They were simply expressing the implications of their understanding of God for the future. It was then the Christian Church which recognized in the coming of Christ events which seemed to them to fulfil the prophetic hopes and promises. To these, as to the threats, we shall return later in this book.

Earlier this century scholars tended to regard the prophets as the founders of an Israelite religion which was quite distinct from other religions of the same day and age. They were working on the assumption that the books of the Law (Genesis to Deuteronomy) were written later than the prophets and therefore owed a great deal to their teaching. More recent scholarship has found that much of the material in those first five books of the Old Testament is quite ancient, having been preserved for many generations orally, even if some of it had not been written down until the period of the prophets.[3] But some of it would already have been known in written form also by the middle of the 9th century when the classical prophets emerged. Therefore the prophets are to be seen not so much as innovators but rather as preachers who base their message on existing traditions, either by criticizing the way they have been understood or breathing new life into them when they had become fossilized.

Further the prophets used to be regarded as unique to Israel. Once again this is not wholly wrong, for nowhere else do we find men who can be compared with the great prophetic figures of the Old Testament. But more recent discoveries and studies have shown that in many other cultures, eastern and western, ancient and more modern, there are men and women who are not altogether unlike the Old Testament prophets. It is just as easy to make too much of these similarities as it is to make too little of them. When all has been said and done the 'classical' prophets of the Old Testament whose words have been preserved for us in the prophetic books do stand out as different from all other characters however similar they may seem superficially. From beginnings which were similar to those outside Israel Old Testament prophecy grew into something quite distinctive.

Several examples of this kind of religious person have been

collected together by J. Lindblom.[4] He enumerates a number of characteristics which enable us to describe a person as prophetic[5] and then uses this as a kind of check-list against which certain individuals and groups of people may be examined. They must be wholly devoted to the god whom they worship; they are inspired and under divine constraints showing signs of ecstasy and abnormal behaviour; they receive revelations from their god and announce them publicly; they have a special call from the deity to fulfil his purpose unconditionally. This would be a fair enough description of the Israelite prophets, but Lindblom goes on to show how groups outside Israel also fulfil these conditions. We too may look at one or two groups of people living in the Ancient Near East in the years between 2000 BC and 500 BC.

We turn first to the kingdom of Mari in Northern Mesopotamia which reached its high point about 1700 BC. This was the area from which some of Israel's ancestors came and the Old Testament tells how both Isaac and Jacob travelled back there to find their wives. (Gen. 25:20, 28:14). In AD 1933 André Parrot, a French archaeologist, unearthed some 20,000 clay tablets in the palace buildings of the king, Zimri-lin. These have thrown new light on many Old Testament passages. Among them were several tablets which contained references to men who, in some respects, seem to be similar to Israelite prophets.[6] One tells of a man called Malik who had a dream in which he received a message from the god Dagon. He was to announce this message to the governor who would pass it on to king Zimri-lin. The message called upon Zimri-lin to be obedient to Dagon who would in return grant him victories over the 'men of the South'[7] This account of a god sending a message to a king through another man reminds us of several Old Testament stories of prophets. Micaiah had a message from Yahweh for Ahab in 1 Kings 22. Elijah, too, received messages for Ahab from Yahweh (1 Kings 18 and 21). In the same way Isaiah confronted both Ahaz (Is. 7) and Hezekiah (Is. 37:21 ff.) with a message from Yahweh.

In another tablet the man entrusted with the message is called a *muḫḫum*. He tells the king, 'The god has sent me'. What he has to tell is very different from the messages of the

Old Testament prophets – the king is to make 'sacrifices of the dead', probably human sacrifices, to the dead spirit of his father. All the same the way. the message was conveyed is similar to that in the Old Testament. Elsewhere another *muḫḫum* brought a message from Dagon commanding the king to build a new city gate.

Yet another tablet tells of an *apilum*, meaning 'answerer'. The message is from the god Adad to king Zimri-lin demanding from him a site for a temple, seeing that he has set him on the throne and built him a palace. If this demand were met then Zimri-lin would prosper further; if not, he would lose all he had. This calls to mind the conversation between Nathan and David (2 Samuel 7) which deals differently with the same question. David is told not to build a Temple for Yahweh, though Yahweh will build a house, a dynasty, for David. Any king who disobeys will be punished though the dynasty will continue. In the biblical story the message appears to come to Nathan out of the blue while the Mari text is not clear on this point. There the *apilum* may have been a person connected with the sanctuary who enjoyed the privilege of conversation with the god.

Finally there is a reference to people called *baru*, that is, 'seers'. These people are rather different from either the *muḫḫum* or the *apilum*. Instead of receiving a message from the god and passing it on, they rather seek advice from him by means of omens. Here the similarities with the Old Testament prophets are less obvious.

It is clear from these texts that in an area with which Israel had close connections there were men who, like Israel's prophets, were sent by the gods with a message to the king. In this respect they fulfil certain of the criteria set up by Lindblom. There is no mention of any special call, but we should not be too surprised at this since the texts are all brief and the same could be said of Nathan and Elijah in the Old Testament.

That there were prophets in Phoenicia to the north west of Israel we may be sure from 1 Kings 18 where we read of the prophets of Baal and Asherah. They are, of course, very different from the Israelite prophets. They bring no message from their god but only seek to persuade him, by prayer and by cutting themselves, to do what they want. But the fact that the Old Testament actually calls them prophets indicates that they were sufficiently like the Israelite prophets to be recognized as such. There is also one other piece of evidence from this area. Curiously enough the document is an Egyptian one but it describes events which took place at Byblos in Phoenicia. It is called the *Story of Wen-Amon* and is dated about 1000 BC.

Wen-Amon was an Egyptian who was sent to the port of Byblos to buy timber. While he was there he was robbed of the money with which to pay for it and was therefore detained in the harbour until the thief should be caught. He erected a tent on the beach and hid in it an image of his god, Amon, which he had brought with him on the voyage. During this time the king of Byblos went to his temple to offer sacrifice to Baal. While he was doing so a certain young man fell into an ecstatic trance and it was revealed to him that Wen-Amon had brought an image of Amon with him and hidden it in his tent. This information he passed on to the king. The rest of the story doesn't concern us.[8] The important point for our purpose is that a god took possession of a man and revealed secret knowledge to him which he passed on to the king.

There is another Egyptian document even older than the *Story of Wen-Amon*, dated between 2000 and 1750 BC. This one concerns Egypt itself and since it is sometimes called *The Prophecies of Neferte*[9] it must be mentioned here, although the similarities with Israelite prophecy are not strong. The document is a piece of political propaganda supporting the present king. It does so by telling how a much earlier king, Snerfu, was seeking entertainment at his court. His courtiers recommended that a certain wise man or priest called Neferte be invited to entertain. The entertainment consisted of foretelling all the evils and calamities which would take place in Egypt until a new king should come to the throne. Naturally, the 'new king' was the one for whom the document was written. The fore-telling of calamity at once links this with Hebrew prophecy, but there is none of the criteria demanded by Lindblom, no call, no possession, no inspiration. Neferte is much more like a Wise Man than a prophet.

These examples will indicate that in other cultures around

Israel there were men who in some respects resembled the Old Testament prophets and the phenomenon of prophecy may not be unique to Israel. All the same these resemblances remain somewhat rare and superficial. Certainly there is a world of difference between the *muḫḫum* of the Mari texts and an Isaiah or a Jeremiah, and if the texts we have examined throw any light upon the origins of prophecy in Israel, and we shall consider this in the next chapter, they throw no light at all upon Hebrew prophecy in the classical period from the 9th to 5th centuries BC.

2. The Lord's Spokesmen in Early Israel

The similarities and dissimilarities between prophecy in Israel and prophecy as described in writings from Israel's neighbours leaves us with a perplexing problem about the origins of prophecy in Israel. Did Israel 'borrow' it from her neighbours after the settlement in Canaan or was it known already to those tribes who later became Israel before they had settled in the Promised Land? These questions can be answered only very tentatively. G. Von Rad[10] says, 'The origins of prophecy are themselves a difficult problem: there is not enough source material and what there is is not sufficiently homogeneous to allow us to draw up anything like a history of the movement or even a rough sketch of its beginnings.'

Three main views have emerged. First Von Rad himself suggests that in the light of such evidence as we summarized in the last chapter Israel first came into contact with prophecy among Canaanite people after the settlement on Canaanite soil and took it over from them, adapting it in the process to her own conception of God.[11]

Second, W. Eichrodt[12] holds the view that prophecy was not borrowed from anyone but originated naturally in Israel as it had done among other peoples. Often it is associated with abnormal behaviour due to possession by God in which a man ceases temporarily to be himself and becomes 'ecstatic'. Such a state was the outcome of the 'sacred dance'. Dancing as a form of religious expression is found in many cultures and the music and rhythmic movements send the participants into this ecstatic state. Further the fact that the earlier Israelite prophets wore clothes of camel's hair and ate the fare of the desert seems to suggest that they were strongly opposed to the Canaanite way of life and if this is so they were unlikely to 'borrow' anything from it. Thus it arose spontaneously among the Israelite tribes.

The third view is a kind of compromise. Lindblom[13] agrees that prophecy arose in Israel spontaneously, just as it did in many other cultures where ecstatic behaviour followed from a close relationship between certain individuals and their god. He points out that such a phenomenon as ecstasy can hardly be 'borrowed' since it is a real experience and not just an imitation of someone else's behaviour. But the forms in which these possessed people expressed themselves as they conveyed their messages from God, and the terms which were applied to them by others, were quite probably derived from the Canaanites among whom they settled.

There are one or two passages in the Old Testament which ought to throw some light upon the origins of prophecy and upon the terminology used to describe it. None is more important than 1 Samuel 9:9. The verse is obviously a parenthetical note by the compiler of the book, the so-called Deuteronomist historian writing during the exile in Babylon between 587 and 538 BC, in which he seeks, for the benefit of his readers, to explain the word for 'prophet' in the source he was using. The man previously called a seer (Hebrew, *ro'eh*) is now called a prophet (*nabi'*). The word 'seer' is simply the participle of the word meaning 'to see' in the very ordinary sense, but here it refers to Samuel, the man of God, who possesses secret information about the whereabouts of Saul's father's asses and is consulted by Saul so that the information may be passed on to him. It does not refer here to the man who suddenly receives information from God 'out of the blue' and passes it on to another. However, the editor now identifies Samuel as a prophet, using the term *nabi'*, which, by the time of the exile, has become a technical term for a prophet. Two possible explanations have been offered for the inclusion of this explanatory note. First, 1 Samuel is made up of different sources brought together by the editor. Those underlying chapters 1–3 called Samuel a *nabi'* (3:20) whereas those underlying chapter 9 regard him as a *ro'eh* or a man of God. The note therefore is the attempt of the final editor to reconcile the terminology in his two sources.[14] Alternatively, it may reflect a real change of terminology in the course of time,

10

suggesting that in early Israel there were professional 'seers', people who sought information from God and were paid for doing so, but gradually these were replaced by 'prophets'. The editor is then forging a link between these two groups of people.[15]

In any case the seer is presented to us as a man who knows secret things and can reveal these to others. He receives payment for his services (v. 9), is closely associated with worship at the sanctuary and the sacrificial feast cannot begin until he has blessed the sacrifice (v. 12). So he has a priestly function as well. In these respects he is not unlike the *baru* of the Mari texts and, more generally, the 'diviners' of the Ancient Near East. This is not to say that the seer is identical with the diviner of the Old Testament for the latter is designated by a different Hebrew word and is usually condemned by the prophets (Is. 3.3). Yet his function is not wholly dissimilar.

The term 'seer' is applied again to Balaam in Numbers 22–24. These chapters contain a number of very curious stories, but we need not stay to discuss them now in detail. Balak, the king of Moab, sent Balaam to curse Israel, making payment to him for this 'divination'. Balaam, however, received a message from Israel's God reminding him that he could not curse what Yahweh had blessed. On his way back to Balak he received a vision from Yahweh – an angel confronted the ass upon which he was riding – and again he was told that he could only say that Yahweh had told him to say. Divination and charms were powerless against Israel once Yahweh had blessed her. In 24:16 he is described as a man who sees visions and hears the word of God which he cannot deny. Thus inspired by the 'spirit of Yahweh' he utters God's word. Balaam, then, is presented as a 'seer', a cultic person who has visions, practises divination and utters curses. But on this occasion he feels himself under divine constraint through the spirit of God to speak the word which God gives him to speak. It may be that the account of a 'seer' has been transformed by the theological reflection of the editor into an account of a 'prophet'. At the same time it should be remembered that in some of the examples given in chapter 1 above the two roles are found side by side in the same person.

11

There is also another Hebrew word which may be translated 'seer'. It is derived from a verb (*hazah*) which tends to indicate seeing a vision as well as seeing literally with the eyes. This term is applied to 'the prophet Gad, David's seer' in 2 Samuel 24:11. Here the words prophet and seer are used synonymously. Clearly at some point all three words, *ro'eh*, *hozeh* and *nabi'* could all be used to describe the same kind of person.

In the days of the Judges the feminine form of the word *nabi'* is used to describe Deborah, but it is hard to see what kind of activity she engaged in which could earn her that title. The fact that she used to sit under the palm tree and people came to her for judgement may suggest something of the function of the 'seer'. W. Eichrodt[16] had suggested that she is described here 'in the language of a later time', but even if that is so the traditions about her must have been sufficiently 'prophetic' to justify calling her a prophetess. Perhaps it was her almost fanatical zeal for Yahweh which also earned her the title since this was certainly a characteristic of the later prophets in the time of Elijah.

The term *nabi'* comes to the fore in the stories about Saul in 1 Samuel 10. Here Saul falls in with a band of prophets (*nebi'im*) as they are coming down from the 'high place', that is, the sanctuary where in all probability they had been participating in worship. As often in this early period they are found in a group and not as individuals (cf. 1 Sam. 19:20, 1 Kings 22:6). They prophesy to the accompaniment of musical instruments and almost certainly these are intended to stimulate a state of mind and body to which the term ecstasy is usually applied. Very likely this involved some rhythmic dancing movement in which they were no longer in control of themselves but were possessed by forces from outside themselves. We are not told in this account exactly what the ecstatic behaviour was, but clearly there was something about them which made them recognizable as prophets. When he met them Saul also was caught up in the same experience and this is described by saying that Saul was 'turned into another man'. He was no longer himself. This was brought about by the 'spirit of God'. The meeting with the prophets was a sign to Saul confirming the word of promise which God had spoken to him. From now on he was under divine constraint and God promised to be with him. All this corresponds with the definition of ecstasy given by Lindblom, as 'an abnormal state of consciousness in which one is so intensely absorbed by one single idea or one single feeling, or by a group of ideas or feelings, that the normal stream of psychical life is more or less arrested. The bodily senses cease to function; one becomes impervious to impressions from without; consciousness is exalted above the ordinary level of daily experience; unconscious mental impressions and ideas come to the surface in the form of visions and auditions'.[17] In this account, then, of events in the very earliest days of the Hebrew monarchy we are given a glimpse of a group of ecstatic prophets, inspired by the spirit of God.

There is one account of prophetic activity from an even earlier period. Numbers 11:10ff. describes certain events as taking place during the period of the wilderness wanderings. If this is taken purely at its face value we should have to say that the Israelites knew and experienced prophecy before they entered Canaan and did not in any way borrow it from the Canaanites. Many regard these stories as aetiological accounts, that is, stories which seek to explain the origin of some phenomenon. Lindblom[18] thinks there are two such narratives, the first accounting for the institution of the elder-ship, the second accounting for that of prophecy. Both of these were familiar in later Israel. The elders feature in such passages as Exodus 24:1, Joshua 24:1, Ezekiel 8:1, Ezra 10:8. The present passage in Numbers seeks to show how important they were and how much to be respected because they shared the inspiration of Moses himself, the spirit of Yahweh which was with him being shared now with them. Since Moses was later known as a prophet those who shared his inspiration were also called prophets. Suspicion is surely aroused that something like this is the explanation of the story by the fact that they are said to have prophesied this once and then no more and we are not told what the purpose of their prophesying was.

It seems that the narrator knew very well that prophecy was only known in Israel after the settlement in Canaan. The second narrative in vv. 26-30 indicates that when Israel did

13

come face to face with prophecy there was considerable opposition to it. It does so by presenting Joshua as rejecting it. But Moses supported it and, because of his attitude to it, it became accepted in Israel. If this is so then, of course, the stories have no historical value and say nothing about the origins or history of prophecy in the wilderness period, but only reflect later attitudes to it. Von Rad,[19] too, sees this as a 'comparatively late tradition' and as evidence of Israel's encounter with this phenomenon of prophecy, an encounter in which they did not know what to make of it, but eventually accepted it after a good deal of hesitancy and perplexity.

Between these early stories and the time of the later 'classical' prophets we have stories of individuals and groups in the 9th century BC. Elijah himself always appears as an individual, not apparently associated with a group. He is recognized as a figure of some importance by another prophet, Obadiah, who himself belonged to a group of prophets who were being persecuted by Jezebel (1 Kings 18:7ff.). He appears quite suddenly to confront both Ahab the king and the people with a message from God. Elisha (2 Kings 1–9) is a slightly different kind of figure. Many of the stories concerning him are variants of those told about Elijah but he does appear as the leader of a group with whom he shares his meals (2 Kings 4:38f.). King Ahab has his own group of prophets at court (1 Kings 22) who tell him exactly what he wishes to hear, yet out of this group there stands one Micaiah who has a different message. Instead of the customary message promising success he has a real message from God which threatens Ahab with defeat and death. In this case the group and the individual are at variance and the individual is the one whose message is fulfilled. So by this time we begin to get not only the group phenomenon but also certain individual prophets who appear with a different message and it is clear that these two forms of prophecy continue at least until the exile in Babylon.

So we may begin to list certain features of early prophecy. Prophets were inspired by the spirit of God (1 Sam. 10:6, 18:12, 19:18ff.) or empowered by the 'hand of God' (1 Kings 18:46). By this they became ecstatic (1 Sam. 10:5, 19:22-24, 1 Kings 22:10, 18:46), possibly going into a trance (2 Kings

14

8:7ff.). In this condition they had visions (1 Kings 22, 2 Kings 6) and became clairvoyant (1 Sam. 10, 1 Kings 13:1ff., 14, 17:1, 2 Kings 1:2ff., 6:9ff.). Some performed miracles (2 Kings 1–9, the stories of Elisha especially). They spoke the word of God (1 Kings 14:1–18, 22:14) using parables (2 Sam. 12) or symbolic actions (1 Kings 22:11, 2 Kings 13:14ff.). This is not an attempt to build up an identikit picture of a prophet but to collect together some of the things said about them in this period.

3. Called to be a Prophet

One of the criteria listed by Lindblom[20] by which to recognize a prophet was the special call to proclaim the word of the god unconditionally. But we have already seen that often both within the Old Testament and outside it the narratives about prophets are too brief for any such call to be described. In some of the prophetic books of the Old Testament, however, we do find descriptions of a call and it will be well now to look at these to see whether we can discover how a man came to be a prophet and what were the consequences of this for him.

Before we do so there are one or two other points to be raised. First, the only call narratives which are left to us are those of Isaiah, Jeremiah, Ezekiel, Hosea, probably Amos and possibly Second Isaiah, the prophet of the exile whose words are contained in Isaiah 40–55. None is to be found in the books of Joel, Obadiah, Micah, Nahum, Zephaniah, Haggai, Zechariah or Malachi. The case of Habakkuk depends upon the interpretation of chapter 2. In these latter books we have the simple statements, found also in the other prophetic books, that 'the word came to me' or 'I saw the word' or 'I saw a vision'. It may be that the call narratives have been preserved only in the larger books, but it does leave open the question of how these men came to regard themselves and to be regarded as prophets.

Second, we have to ask ourselves how the accounts of the calls have come to us. We shall discuss more fully later how the prophetic words became prophetic books[21] but we can say now that it is very unlikely that the prophets wrote down their experiences and words themselves. That being so, we must assume that they related their call experiences to others, be they friends or disciples, at some time later than the call itself. It is not unlikely therefore that the accounts contain a certain degree of theological reflection and interpretation in the light of subsequent events. On the other hand, the accounts are

16

generally very restrained and show no signs of having been exaggerated in order to make them more spectacular. Still, it is these other people, who also collected and edited the prophets' words, who wrote down the call narratives and some allowance may have to be made for their point of view. But, again, a close examination of the narratives provides little evidence of this. Even in the book of Jeremiah which was very thoroughly edited by the Deuteronomists during the exile[22] editorial activity is not very obvious in the call narrative in chapter 1. We may therefore accept them as accounts coming from the prophet himself, preserved and passed on by people who were close to him and to whom he had confided a description of his experience.

Only in the case of Ezekiel do we find any concentration upon the phenomena associated with the call. Elsewhere the experience is subordinate to the message which is given to the prophet to proclaim and it is upon the content of the preaching that the emphasis falls. The experience itself is important only in so far as it is the vehicle for this message. Even in Ezekiel the fuller description of the vision he has serves only to underline the deeper understanding of God which has come to him through it.

From such biographical or autobiographical passages as we possess we can see that the prophets were men of very different types. Amos was a herdsman and a dresser of sycamore figs, who worked in the wilderness of Tekoa in Judah (1:1, 7:14). Yet we must not think of him as an ignorant peasant, for he is well informed about current affairs and about events in the world around Israel, both past and present. Though a Judaean his ministry is to be performed in the Northern Kingdom of Israel. That ministry, as far as our records tell us, was a brief one.

Hosea, on the other hand was himself an Israelite speaking to Israelites. The only information we have about him is found in chapters 1–3 and there is some doubt as to whether these chapters are to be seen as literal descriptions of his marital experience and what is the relationship between chapters 1 and 3. Somewhat different views of his call experience, therefore, emerge depending upon the interpretation of these chapters. Isaiah, like Amos a Judaean, seems to belong to the upper classes in Jerusalem. He has access to the king; he is familiar with the Temple and its services; he is familiar with the teaching of the Wise Men who are to be found in the Jerusalem court. He was married with children. We are not told what his occupation was, but his prophetic ministry lasted for some forty or more years.

Micah, on the other hand, was a country man from Judah and therefore, though contemporary with Isaiah, looks at things from a slightly different point of view. Jeremiah, who lived a century later, belonged to a family which had priestly connections. His home town of Anathoth was on the border between Israel and Judah. His ministry in Judah brought him into conflict not only with the authorities there but with his own family. By family we mean parents and brothers, for he was forbidden to marry and have children himself. Ezekiel was actually a priest who was now called to be a prophet. He found himself in exile in Babylon and had his call there. Much of his teaching, therefore, is directed to his fellow-exiles. Zechariah too may well have been of a priestly family (Neh. 12:4), while Nahum was very likely a professional or court prophet, that is, a member of a prophetic group associated with the king's court out of which he was called to make his own individual assessment of the fate of Assyria.

One thing that the prophets have in common is that their ministries were undertaken at critical moments in the political and religious history of their people. Amos and Hosea both prophesied in the final days of the Northern Kingdom of Israel, shortly before its decimation by the Assyrians. Isaiah and Micah both recognize the threat to Judah posed by these same Assyrians. They seem to disagree about the outcome, as to whether the Assyrians will now capture Jerusalem or not. Jeremiah and Ezekiel are both concerned with the events surrounding the downfall of Jerusalem, the temple and the Jewish nation, a shattering experience for all concerned. Second Isaiah looks forward to the imminent return of the exiles to their homeland, while Haggai and Zechariah prophesy soon after that return has taken place. So God's call comes to a variety of men who are given the task of declaring the will and purpose of God in the crises which their nations face.

The call itself comes in a variety of ways. Amos (Amos

7:1-9) and Jeremiah (Jer. 1:11-14) both see familiar things around them which, under the inspiration of God, suddenly become significant for them, a swarm of locusts, a man with a plumb-line, a basket of summer fruit, a rod of almond blossom or a boiling pot. The sight of the *qayis* (summer fruit) assures Amos that the *qes* (end) is coming. While for Jeremiah the sight of a *šaqed* (almond bough) indicates to him that God is *šoqed* (watching over) his word to perform it. Isaiah's vision comes to him, apparently while he is in the temple and the familiar things there take on new significance for him, the external surroundings becoming the means of an inner experience. If the early chapters of Hosea do tell us something about the prophet's family life then the personal tragedy of his home life provides him with the message about the relationship between Yahweh and Israel. In a similar way, half way through his ministry, Ezekiel comes to regard the death of his wife as a message from God about the fate of Jerusalem. He is forbidden to mourn her death because of this greater tragedy which is to befall Judah. His initial call however, appears to be purely visionary. Similarly the opening verse of Nahum speaks of a vision, without in any way describing it.

Consequently the call is a very personal experience closely related to the prophet's own circumstances. Amos and Jeremiah are both addressed by name, while in the case of Hosea and Ezekiel it is the highly personal relationships of family life which form the background and the basis of their call. Isaiah has to be cleansed and made fit for his task, his own sin being forgiven.

The prophets' response to this call is often one of disbelief, reluctance and a feeling of inadequacy. The recognition of God's holiness in the temple makes Isaiah deeply aware of his own uncleanness which would make it impossible for him properly to serve his God as his mouthpiece. He is too deeply implicated in the sin of his people to be able to address them in the name of the holy God. Jeremiah's hesitancy stems more from his youth and inexperience. How can he who has just about attained manhood proclaim a message which has world wide implications? Ezekiel, perhaps even more so than Isaiah, is overwhelmed by the holiness, power and majesty of

God and can only fall prostrate before him. It is not until God calls him to stand on his feet that he is able to hear and proclaim the message which God is giving to him.

It is this feeling of inadequacy which keeps the prophets aware of the power of God and of their dependence upon him throughout their lives. Their ministry is but a part of the great divine purpose in which they, by their call, have been caught up. So Jeremiah sees that he was actually created by God for this very purpose (1:5). He was born for this very moment and destined to this task before his birth. Therefore there was no escape from it. He must declare the will and purpose of God and the very declaration is a part of that purpose. Amos makes the same point in chapter 3. The series of questions has a double climax. One part of it in v. 8 is that when God calls a man to prophesy then the man has really no option. He is caught up into the very purpose of God and must play his part in it by declaring his word.

There is no evidence to suggest that the prophets ever set out to become prophets. What evidence there is suggests the reverse, that God took the initiative in singling out these men for their task and calling them to it. Consequently all through their ministries they were being confronted by the word of God in their varied experiences and only rarely do they seem to have sought it in quiet retreat. Jeremiah 28:11f. may suggest that on one occasion he did so because of his uncertainty in face of contradiction by another prophet. Just as the call came in the real, concrete experience of life so the message was related to the real, concrete events in the life of their nation. Thus there is a subtle combination of what we should call the 'religious' and the 'political'. To put it better, the word which comes to them through outward circumstances is recognized as God's word and must be applied to those circumstances.

The actual message to be proclaimed is not usually set out clearly and in detail in the call. The initial word is quite general (for example, 'the end is coming', Amos 8:2) and this has to be worked out and applied as events move on. The material prosperity of the Northern Kingdom led the Israelites into a state of false security, but because of the message given to him at his call Amos can see beneath the top-soil of prosperity to the seeds of disaster beneath. He may not be clear how the disaster will come, but come it will and he has no other word to proclaim than that the end is coming.

Isaiah, at his call, is given a most curious message to proclaim. His task is to 'harden the people's hearts' and so stop them from repenting until after they have been punished. Here there arises the question raised earlier about the later reflection on the call in the light of subsequent events. Many scholars[23] have suggested that because people did not listen to Isaiah's words during his ministry the account of his call (ch. 6), written later, expressed this result as though it had been God's purpose. More recently,[24] however, the words have been taken quite at their face value as indicating that God intended that Isaiah's task should be to harden the people's hearts, because the sooner this happened, the sooner would punishment befall them and the sooner could his purpose of renewal be fulfilled. So Isaiah pronounces the coming downfall of Israel the Northern Kingdom and it falls. The downfall of the Southern Kingdom of Judah was delayed, getting a temporary reprieve in 701 until 587 BC, but the prophet saw beyond it to a new day in which Yahweh would restore his people and give them a new start.

Jeremiah's task, given to him at his call (Jer. 10), was to 'pluck up and to break down, to destroy and to overthrow, to build and to plant'. Again this message is spelled out in relation to the various events through which he lived – Josiah's reforms, the sieges of Jerusalem in 597 and 587 BC, the murder of Gedeliah. Here too the building can only follow the destruction which must precede it. Hosea's message is given to him in the names he has to give to his children, which indicate that Israel will cease to be the people of God (Hos. 1:4-8). This he proclaims unremittingly, though he also sees hope beyond it. If Isaiah 40:1-5 does provide an account of the prophet's call then he, standing beyond the judgement of the exile, is to proclaim a new future for the Jews back in their home land. The rest of the book is a series of variations upon this theme.

If the call experience gave the prophets the basis of their message it also provided them with a deep sense of compulsion. This is seen particularly clearly in the case of

21

Jeremiah who would dearly have loved to stop preaching and yet was quite unable to do so because of the call of God. The word of God is like a fire within him. He is weary with holding it in and cannot (20:9). Isaiah persists with his message for forty years in spite of the fact that the people pay no heed. Both Amos 3:3-8 and Ezekiel 3 and 33 deal with this matter of prophetic responsibility. The prophet has no option. However distasteful it may be he must proclaim the word of God. It all has to do with the meaning of this phrase the 'word of God', to which we shall turn in the next chapter.

4.   The Hand, Spirit and Word of Yahweh

We have already used these phrases more than once in connection with the prophet's activity and it is now time to look at each in turn.

On several occasions the inspiration of the prophet is said to be due to the 'hand of Yahweh' upon him. This has often been understood to denote the onset of ecstasy.[25] It was the 'hand of Yahweh' which enabled Elijah to run faster than Ahab's chariot from Carmel to Jezreel, a feat which could only be accomplished when in an ecstatic state (1 Kings 18:46). The playing of the minstrel induced the 'hand of Yahweh' upon Elisha and enabled him to prophesy. Since music is used to induce ecstasy the 'hand of Yahweh' here must denote an ecstatic state (2 Kings 3:15). But the phrase is used also of Isaiah (Is. 8:11) and Jeremiah (Jer. 1:8) where there is no suggestion of ecstatic behaviour. It occurs predominantly in the book of Ezekiel (1:3, 3:14, 3:22, 8:1, 8:3, 33:22, 37:1, 40:1) and since Ezekiel does manifest what looks like ecstatic behaviour on a number of occasions the suggestion that 'hand of Yahweh' refers to the onset of ecstasy seems well founded. However, it would be wrong to separate the use of the phrase in the prophetic context from its use elsewhere and it occurs no less than 122 times altogether in the Old Testament.

Now the Hebrew uses the names of parts of the body not only to denote a physical feature but also to indicate the function which that physical feature performs.[26] A hand, then, is not just the part of the body at the end of the arm; it is also power. We use the words in exactly the same way in English in such phrases as 'you're in my hands'. So the 'hand of Yahweh' denotes his power in punishment (Exod. 3:20, Is. 5:25ff., Ezek. 6:14), in deliverance (Exod. 13:3, Deut. 7:8, Ps.

23

109:27), in creation (Job 10:8, Ps. 8:6, Ps. 95:4f.), in providence (Job 12:9, Ps. 95:7, Ps. 104:28), in care and protection (2 Sam. 24:14, Ps. 31:5, Ps. 73:23). We should deduce from this that when it occurs with reference to the prophets it simply means the power to fulfil their calling and to prophesy. Sometimes this may involve ecstasy, sometimes not. It is the power which enables Elijah to run faster than Ahab's chariot and which enables Elisha, Isaiah, Jeremiah and Ezekiel to prophesy. It does not necessarily mean that they did so in an ecstatic state. The 'hand of Yahweh', then, denotes simply the empowering of the prophet.

The 'spirit of Yahweh' also speaks of his power and it is no accident that hand and spirit occur together in a number of places (Ezek. 3:14, 3:22ff., 8:1-3, 37:1). A full examination of the use of the phrase 'spirit of Yahweh' is beyond the scope of this chapter and so a few examples of its use must suffice. In Exodus 35:30f. Bezalel is a skilled craftsman because he has been called by God and the spirit of God is upon him. The spirit of Yahweh enables Jephthah to defeat the Ammonites (Jud. 11:29) and it clothes Gideon enabling him to become the leader of the Hebrew tribes (Jud. 6:34). Samson was able to tear a lion apart with his bare hands because the spirit of Yahweh was upon him (Jud. 14:6). When the spirit departed from Saul and came upon David the former lost his power to rule and the latter gained it (1 Sam. 16:13). Similarly the ideal ruler anticipated by Isaiah is enabled to rule perfectly because he is endowed with the spirit of Yahweh (Is. 11). The servant of Yahweh in Isaiah 42:1, whoever he may be, is enabled to fulfil his task, whether it be royal or prophetic,[27] because the spirit of Yahweh is upon him. In precisely the same way it is the spirit of God which enables Saul to prophesy in 1 Samuel 10:6 as well as Saul's messengers to Samuel in 1 Samuel 19:18ff. It empowers Ezekiel not only to prophesy but to have visions of what is happening in Judah while he is in Babylon (Ezek. 8:1). Sometimes we may infer from the context that ecstasy is involved. In 1 Samuel 19:18ff. Saul sends three lots of messengers to Samuel and David at Naioth in Ramah. When they arrive and see Samuel prophesying the spirit falls on them and they also prophesy and the same happens when Saul comes himself. The story clearly implies

24

that there was some external, visible phenomenon, such as ecstasy, which was easily recognizable by the onlooker. But it is the context and the whole story which implies this rather than the phrase 'spirit of God' on its own and we must not infer that the phrase always denotes ecstasy.

One further point about the spirit of God. The Hebrew word also means 'wind' and it seems to carry with it the notion of unpredictability (cf. John 3:8) as well as power. It therefore underlines the points we have made already that it is impossible to say in advance who will become a prophet or who will not. The choice and the empowering is due entirely to God and there can be no true prophet without both of these.

If 'hand' and 'spirit' speak of the means of inspiration 'word of Yahweh' speaks rather of the content of prophecy, but, as was hinted at the end of the last chapter, this phrase is somewhat richer in Hebrew than the corresponding one in English, for the Hebrew word *dabar* indicates not only the word spoken but the deed done which that spoken word describes. We may see this very clearly in the various Old Testament statements about creation. In Gen. 1 God said, 'let there be ...' and 'there was ...'. Here the speaking of the word causes what is spoken to happen. Similarly in Psalm 33:6 the heavens were made simply by the word of Yahweh. Cf. also Psalm 148:5, Amos 9:6, Jonah 4:6, Isaiah 41:4, 45:12, 48:13. The 'word', then, is powerful, effective, dynamic and accomplishes what it describes.

All this has to be borne in mind when speaking of the 'word of Yahweh' which the prophets uttered.[28] It was not an idle word, nor merely a description of something they believed would happen. It was the word of Yahweh. If Yahweh had spoken it then without doubt what he had spoken would come about, later if not sooner. The word would not lose its dynamic until it had been fulfilled. It goes forth from Yahweh's mouth and will not return empty, unfulfilled, but will accomplish what God intended when he spoke it (Is. 55:11). The prophet's task was to hear this word and to repeat it, for in speaking it again he was helping it towards its fulfilment. The story in 1 Kings 22 well illustrates the point. Ahab's prophets claim that they have heard the 'word of

Yahweh' and that the king will be victorious in the battle he wishes to fight against the Syrians. But Micaiah says they have got it wrong. This is not the 'word of Yahweh'. He has heard it and the true word of Yahweh is that if Ahab goes to war then Israel will be left as 'sheep without a shepherd', that is, the king will be killed and Israel defeated. Ahab accepts the views of the other prophets but as an insurance against the word proclaimed by Micaiah he disguises himself as an ordinary soldier so that the Syrians will not pick him out and kill him. 'But a certain man drew his bow at a venture' and without realizing it killed the king of Israel. All the human efforts in the world cannot thwart the word of God. It pursues its way unerringly towards its fulfilment and the proclamation of it by a prophet simply helps it on its way.

This word of Yahweh may be a word of comfort and consolation as it is in Isaiah 40-55, but far more frequently it is a word of judgement upon Israel or Judah or even upon foreign nations. In the latter case one may imagine the prophets enjoying the task of impelling the word of judgement forward. But when it was directed against their own nations and their fellow countrymen and, more particularly, against the chosen people of God then it went against the grain to have to utter it and so help to bring it about. Yet this is what they had to do. This is why there was such a sense of compulsion as we have already seen in the case of Jeremiah (20:9).

Anyone at all familiar with the prophetic books will know the formula by which many prophetic sayings are introduced, 'Thus saith the LORD.' This so-called 'messenger formula'[29] is better translated, 'This is what the LORD has said.' God has spoken his word; the prophet, as the messenger of God, has heard it and must now pass on the message to the people for whom it is intended, speeding the Lord's word on its way.

Sometimes, indeed often, there is a distinction between Yahweh's word and the prophet's own word.[30] This can be seen in such passages as Amos 5:1-3. In the first two verses Amos himself describes the situation as he sees it in a lamentation 'Fallen, no more to rise, is the virgin Israel; forsaken on her land, with none to raise her up.' Into this situation he then injects the word of Yahweh with the messenger formula, 'This is what the LORD has said' and goes on to threaten the deci-

26

mation of the Israelite armies. Further examples can be found in Isaiah 1:21-23 and 24-26 and again in Isaiah 18:1-3 and 4. This means that the prophet is not simply the unthinking mouthpiece of Yahweh. His own personality and consciousness play their part in his work. Into his own reflections about the contemporary situation he injects the 'word of Yahweh'.

It is important to remember that it is Yahweh who speaks first, the prophet echoing his word. Consequently, for all the power that there is in the word of the prophet, it is never magical in its effects. It can never compel Yahweh to act. The prophet is utterly dependent upon Yahweh and if he hears no word he has nothing to say. What he must do is 'stand in the counsel of God' (Jer. 23:18) and wait for God to speak. Only then can he stand before the people and declare to them the 'word of the LORD'.

5. Prophetic Action and Popular Reaction

Many of the prophets were called upon not only to speak the word of God but in some way to embody that word in personal action. It is hard to find a phrase which will adequately describe these actions. Sometimes phrases like 'prophetic symbolism' or 'symbolic action'[31] are used and will serve provided we understand the term 'symbol' as something more than an illustrative sign which gives added point to a verbal message, for these actions are much more than early visual aids.

Others have used the phrase 'sympathetic magic'[32] or 'imitative magic'. In the study of religions this means the performance of an act which imitates the action the worshipper wants his god to perform and which compels the god so to act. But in Israel the action is no more magical than the word itself. There are one or two actions by the prophets which could be thought of as magical and indeed in the earliest form of the stories they may have been, but in their present Old Testament context this is no longer so. Underlying the story of Elijah on Mount Carmel there may be a picture of the prophet as a kind of rain-maker (1 Kings 18). Certainly the contest took place in a time of drought and the pouring of water round the altar may have been meant to ensure the coming of rain. This motif, however, is now obscured in the present form of the story, where both the fire in v. 38 and the rain in v. 45 are due solely to the will of God, whose messenger Elijah is. The term 'sympathetic magic' is not therefore very suitable. On the whole it seems better to stick to a more neutral phrase like 'prophetic action'.

For a proper understanding of this we have to go back to our view of the prophetic word as the echo of the word already spoken by God. It will be recalled that the Hebrew word *dabar* means both 'word' and 'deed'.[33] The prophetic action is therefore a *dabar*, a happening, a word in motion. But it no more compels God to act than does the prophetic word. It echoes visibly the will of God just as the word echoes it orally, and so it fulfils the same function as the word. Elijah's pouring of water is thus neither a piece of magic nor a prayer. It is an action which is a part of the whole process by which God's will becomes God's act.

When Ahab consulted his prophets about the battle against the Syrians (1 Kings 22) Zedekiah not only promised him success but made himself a pair of horns and apparently appeared before Ahab wearing them. This action was accompanied by an interpretative word, 'With these you shall push the Syrians until they are destroyed.' Though the prophet is mistaken, the word and the action go together as the expression of what he believes to be the will of God and in this way he seeks to further it.

According to Isaiah 20 the prophet Isaiah had walked about in Jerusalem for three years wearing nothing at all. In view of the Jews' ideas concerning nakedness this is surely not meant to be taken strictly literally, but rather indicates that he wore only the garb of a captive, nothing but a loin cloth, when he appeared in public. There is no suggestion that Isaiah ever explained why he was doing this, but at the end of the period, when the Assyrians were marching through the land and the people of Judah were looking to Egypt for help, the meaning of the prophetic sign became clear to them. Egypt would be taken captive by Assyria and therefore could not be relied upon by the Judaeans for help. If this should happen to the Egyptians upon whom they had relied what would then happen to them? Consistently Isaiah advised reliance upon Yahweh alone and sought to dissuade his people from relying upon any kind of foreign help. His action here is a part of this divine message. Both proclamation and action are a part of the divinely ordained process which is set in motion by the word and the will of God.

Like Zedekiah in 1 Kings 22 Jeremiah, too, is told to wear a wooden yoke (Jer. 27:28). In this new context, however, the yoke has a different meaning. Here it symbolizes the power and authority of Babylon over Judah and the surrounding states and declares God's will that they should submit to the Babylonians. Another contemporary of Jeremiah's, a prophet called Hananiah, then broke the yoke from Jeremiah's shoulders. This, too, was a prophetic act signifying his belief that he had heard the word of God saying that the Babylonian yoke would be removed. Jeremiah now had to consider carefully whether he or Hananiah had heard correctly the true word of God and after a while he came to the conclusion that he had. According to the Hebrew text which is followed by the NEB Jeremiah is now told to make for himself an iron yoke, thus reaffirming his message with a further prophetic act. The Greek text which is followed by the RSV is slightly different in that it reports the word of God to Jeremiah as saying that God will make an iron yoke. It does not see this as a further prophetic act. In this story it is important to realize that the dispute is not simply a dispute between two people as to what was going to happen in the future. It was a very critical matter of understanding what God had already decided to do and had, in fact, begun to do by uttering his word, so that they could help forward his purpose by announcing his word. Subsequent events showed that Jeremiah had heard the word of God correctly, but both here and in Deuteronomy 13 the problem of knowing which of two prophets really had heard and understood the word of God is acknowledged.

It is, however, in the book of Ezekiel that we read more often of these prophetic actions. Perhaps we ought to take more seriously than is often done the statement in 3:26 that soon after his call Ezekiel was struck dumb. Many commentators say that this cannot be taken literally.[34] Others say that it must come from a later period in his life, nearer the fall of Jerusalem and not at his call,[35] or that it is an editorial comment at the time of compiling the book.[36] Certainly it is hard to think of a prophet being struck dumb at the moment he is called to declare the word of God. Yet it is surely no accident that this account of his dumbness is followed in 4:1-5:4 by a series of prophetic actions which contain no verbal proclamation. We are told that he lay on his left side for 390 days and on his right side for 40 days signifying the punishment of Israel and Judah respectively. During this time his food and drink were strictly rationed. The meaning of this action commanded by God is made clear to Ezekiel himself but there is no indication that he put its meaning into words for the benefit of the people who watched him. He also took a brick and drew on it a 'picture' or representation of Jerusalem and then portrayed the siege of the city by means of a kind of 'war game'. Further he shaved off his hair and his beard. One third he burnt, one third he cut up with a sword and one third he scattered to the wind; a few hairs he preserved and tied to his girdle. All these actions are left to speak for themselves. As surely as if he had spoken the word the actions declare it and so help to bring it to pass.

These examples will be sufficient to show how the prophets could, in certain circumstances, either replace or reinforce the spoken word by means of actions. Both word and action were proclamation of the divine word spoken by God and assisted that word on its way towards its fulfilment.

But this speaking or acting of the divine word is not without its difficulties for many of the prophets. In the first place it is difficult and painful to proclaim and so to effect the word of judgement because the prophet himself is one of the people to be judged. This is not always the case, of course. Amos, being a Judaean, was not personally involved in the downfall of Israel. Ezekiel, being in exile already, was spared the fate of being in the city of Jerusalem when it was destroyed by Nebuchadnezzar. On the other hand, Jeremiah was very much involved in the events surrounding the fall of Jerusalem and even when he was offered the chance to leave in 597 BC stayed on to share in the downfall of the city and in the fate of his people. This sense of oneness with his people is seen very clearly in the call of Isaiah when he sees himself as a 'man of unclean lips' dwelling 'among a people of unclean lips'. As a member of sinful Judah he shares their guilt, whether or not he was personally guilty. Although he was forgiven there is no reason to suppose that he was thereby guaranteed any immunity from the disaster which then threatened the land. Some scholars do find in the book of Isaiah references to a 'righteous remnant' which will be saved from the coming disaster and they see the prophet as creating this remnant and therefore belonging to it.[37] More likely, however, when he speaks of a remnant he means nothing more than the few people who will happen to escape the disaster and he is stressing the magnitude and enormity of the disaster rather than any hope for a righteous remnant. The disaster will be so great that hardly anyone will escape.

It is not so much personal danger to themselves which causes anxiety to the prophets; it is the danger to the chosen people of God, the people of which they themselves are an inalienable part. So, for all the harshness of their message there is often a sympathy with their people which makes it hard to proclaim it. When Isaiah is given the task of hardening the people's hearts in chapter 6 his question, 'how long?' is not simply a request for information; it is the traditional opening of a lament as, for instance, in Psalm 79:5. There is here a hint of the burden which his message places upon him. Hosea's prophecies of disaster are among the most vivid and violent of all the prophets and yet it is hard to resist the feeling that when he cries, 'How can I cast you off, O Israel?' (11:8) he is not only proclaiming a word of God but is also expressing his own personal feelings in that word. Here is a tension which must have been hard to bear. Even Amos for whom, as we have seen, the message of the destruction of Israel seems to present few problems because he is a Judaean and not a northern Israelite, pleads for 'Jacob', that is, Israel, with the result that the judgement is postponed.

This tension is particularly strong in the book of Jeremiah. Lack of response from the people he wants to help and the inevitable judgement of his own people cause him great stress. The book of Jeremiah presents us with a much clearer picture of the prophet's own personal life and experience than any other prophetic book. But we have to be a little careful in using it for it is becoming increasingly clear that the book in its present form is the result of a process of editing by people known as the Deuteronomists who, during the exile in Babylon, collected and edited the prophetic material.[38] Their hand can be seen especially clearly in Jeremiah, and the prose sections which tell of his life and experience are heavily coloured by their language and their ideas. Even the auto-biographical material such as the so-called confessions in 11:18-23, 12:1-6, 15:10-21, 17:12-18, 18:18-23, 20:7-18

32

may bear the impress of their teaching. All the same, there is enough to show that Jeremiah suffered greatly from the stress involved in proclaiming a message which he did not want to proclaim and which people did not want to hear. It isolated him from his fellows and so caused him 'pain unceasing' and a 'wound incurable' (15:17f.).

According to chapter 26 we are told that when, in 609 BC, soon after the untimely death of Josiah and the accession of Jehoiakim, he proclaimed the destruction of Jerusalem and the temple his life was seriously threatened and it was only through the intervention of some friends at court that he was spared. In this he was apparently more fortunate than his contemporary Uriah (26:20ff.) who had prophesied similarly. He was forced to flee to Egypt to try to escape persecution, but was eventually brought back and put to death. By this time any prophet who expressed words which might be interpreted as defeatism was in danger of being killed for fear he should spread alarm and despondency. Though Jeremiah escaped death, thanks to his friends, the family of Shaphan, he nevertheless underwent persecution (17:18) and the leaders in Jerusalem plotted against him (18:18ff.). Passhur the priest had him put in the stocks (20:1f.) and this provides the occasion for one of the confessions in which he rebels against his task and yet is unable to refuse it. He can only pray for deliverance from his persecutors. Later, in 597 BC he had to go into hiding (ch. 36) and after the first attack of Jerusalem in that year he was in and out of prison and detention of one sort or another many times until the second attack and the destruction of the city in 587 BC. So we are presented with a clear picture of a prophet who suffers mentally and physically as a result of his prophesying.

Though the picture is especially clear in Jeremiah we should never forget those prophets who were attacked and put to death by Jezebel (1 Kings 18:7ff.), and Elijah himself who was forced to flee from Jezebel (1 Kings 19). Even Amos was turned out of Bethel by Amaziah the priest for prophesying there and forbidden to enter Israel again. There arises therefore a certain tradition about prophetic suffering[39] which may be continued in the quite unsubstantiated story that Isaiah was sawn in two by Manasseh and in the picture of the

Suffering Servant of the Lord in the so-called Servant Songs of Isaiah 40-55.

Finally, both Hosea and Ezekiel have personal experiences which cause them great personal sorrow and suffering and yet which are also prophetic acts. As has been indicated before the relation between chapter 1 and chapter 3 of Hosea is very difficult, as is the interpretation of both chapters.[40] On the whole it is most likely that he had to marry a harlot as a prophetic sign of the unfaithfulness of Israel to Yahweh. If chapter 3 does refer to his re-marriage to Gomer then we have some indication of the shame which it brought to him and the love which he had for the woman. The tension is great, but it is for him only an indication of the great tension in the heart of God himself. In the same way the death of Ezekiel's wife who is the 'light of his eyes' (Ezek. 24:15ff.) is a great personal tragedy made worse by the fact that he is forbidden to mourn her death because this, too, must become a prophetic sign of what God is about to do to Jerusalem and its temple.

The prophets, then, become completely involved in their task in every way. The word of God cannot be separated from the lives they had to live. In one sense it is quite objective, a word which like a self-directing missile finds its way unerringly to its target. Yet on its way it catches up the prophet into its path so that his life and experience become inseparable from it and he is no longer an uninvolved transmitter of the word but a man whose whole personality is bound up with the task of proclamation.

II

Proclamation and Preservation of the Word

6. Times and Places for Speaking

It may come as something of a surprise to the reader that the prophets whose writings are preserved in the Old Testament appeared mainly within the space of 250 years between 750 and 500 BC. Their teaching, therefore, clusters around three main events, the fall of Samaria in 722, the fall of Jerusalem in 587 and the return of some exiles to Jerusalem in 538. The period of classical prophecy is then a short one in comparison with the 1500 years or so between the time of Abraham and Christ. Of course we have seen that there were prophets in Israel at least from the time of Saul before 1000 BC but either the movement was then in an embryonic state or else the collectors of the prophetic material had little interest in what they had said and so did not preserve their words for future generations. We have to allow for the possibility that the concentration on these three events is due to the compilers and that the prophets had more to say about other things and events. On the other hand, we could argue that these were just the sort of circumstances in which God would wish to address his people and that he called the prophets for exactly that purpose.

Whatever our conclusions may be about these questions it is certain that without a clear picture of the history of Israel and Judah between 750 and 500 BC it is hardly possible to understand the prophetic books. The events leading up to and following from the three major experiences of Israel and Judah form the background to the prophets' message and are essential to it. Anyone seeking to hear the prophetic word as it came to the people from the lips of the prophets should read carefully one of the standard histories of this period.[41] The most we can do here is to outline that history and try to show how the prophets related their message to it. Space will allow only the most sketchy outline but this may serve to illustrate the point made in chapter 1 that the prophets were speaking primarily to their own day and age.

Four prophets appeared between 750 and 700, Amos, Hosea, Micah and Isaiah; another four appeared during the following century, Jeremiah, Zephaniah, Nahum and Habakkuk; in the first half of the 6th century we may place Obadiah, Ezekiel and Isaiah 40-55; towards the end of that century come Haggai, Zechariah 1–8, Isaiah 56-66, Joel, Zechariah 9-14 and Malachi. They probably appeared in roughly that order.

By 750 B C the Northern Kingdom of Israel and the Southern Kingdom of Judah were both passing through a time of prosperity. The long reigns of Jeroboam II in the north and Uzziah in the south had helped towards this, but another major factor was that the surrounding nations such as Assyria and Egypt were not particularly strong and therefore had no aspirations on the territories of Palestine or Syria. The economic situation helped to produce a carelessness with regard to religion and a false sense of security. Thus luxurious living forms the background to the prophecies of Amos who condemned not only the luxury itself but also the facile, superficial belief which accompanied it (3:15, 4:1, 6:1-4). Seeing beneath the surface he recognized the religious bankruptcy of Israel, the result of which could only be her punishment by God. As yet, however, he could not discern the instrument God would use to punish her, for the Assyrians did not begin to regain their strength or to renew their aspirations to move westwards until the accession of a king called Tiglath Pileser III in 745. About the same time Jeroboam II died and following him there was a fairly rapid succession of kings on the throne of Israel and one or two revolutions within the next twenty years (2 Kings 15). Hosea is aware of this (7:3-7, 8:4, 13:7-11) and so for him the disintegration of Israel is already beginning and the Assyrians are threatening (5:13). There is no longer any doubt from which direction the punishment will come.

Meanwhile in the kingdom of Judah also the long reign of king Uzziah came to an end about 742[42] and after a brief reign by his son Jotham, Ahaz came to the throne in 735. By this time the Syrians to the north of Israel and the Israelites were alarmed at the threats of Tiglath Pileser and became allies to try to stop his progress westwards. On Ahaz' succession in Judah they invited him to join them, though it was more of a threat than an invitation. This he hesitated to do and so they marched against Jerusalem with the intention of deposing Ahaz and putting a nominee of their own on the throne. It was at this point that Isaiah, who had already followed Amos' example of denouncing the luxury and the lack of true faith in Yahweh, met Ahaz to present him with the 'word of the LORD'. This was a command to take no action at all and wait for the storm to blow over (chs. 7-8). Such advice Ahaz could not follow; instead he asked the Assyrians for help in repelling the coalition ranged against him and so put himself and his country in Assyrian hands. Tiglath Pileser came and punished the Syrians and then the Israelites, as no doubt he would have done even without the invitation of Ahaz.

Damascus fell in 732 and Samaria, the capital of Israel, in 722 BC. Though Isaiah never mentions this event he must have witnessed it from across the border and there may be a hint of it in 28:1-6 where he uses the Israelites as a model for the sin and punishment of Judah. Ahaz died c. 715 BC and was succeeded by Hezekiah during whose reign many of the western states such as Philistia and Edom tried to throw off the Assyrian yoke with the help of Egypt. On more than one occasion he was tempted to join in, and indeed almost certainly did so, though again it was contrary to the continued advice of Isaiah who saw Egyptian help to be useless and pressed Hezekiah to accept the situation as it was until God should change it (chs. 28-31). Because of Hezekiah's rebellion the Assyrians attacked Judah and besieged Jerusalem in 701 BC. This attack is reflected in Isaiah 1:7-8. Isaiah now proclaimed the word of Yahweh that Jerusalem would not, at this time, fall and indeed the siege was lifted and Jerusalem spared (Is. 37:30-35, 2 Kings 19:1-7, 32-37).

Though much less of Micah's teaching has been preserved for us the same background can be discerned. In 1:6 Samaria is still standing, though threatened, while 1:10ff. may well reflect the approach of the Assyrian armies in 701 as in Isaiah 1:7f. The great difference between Isaiah and Micah is that whereas the former sees Jerusalem as about to be spared, the latter sees it as about to be destroyed (3:12). It was not destroyed until 100 years or more later.

The long reign of Manasseh, Hezekiah's son (687–642) was a dark one in which Judah was held in subservience to Assyria. In 640, however, the boy king Josiah came to the throne and by this time the great Assyrian empire was tottering. Supported by Egypt for a while, it finally succumbed to the rising Babylonians in 605. The little state of Judah was caught up in these world events. In 621 there was found a book of the Law in the temple while workmen were busy there carrying out changes to the temple to get rid of Assyrian influence (2 Kings 22). The book gave direction to further reforms through which Josiah demonstrated not only his religious integrity, but also his complete independence from the Assyrians. In 609 he tried to stop the Egyptian army, which was on its way to help the Assyrians, from passing near Judah and at Megiddo he was killed. The Egyptians then put Jehoiakim on the throne and for a while he ruled as their vassal.

In the year of Josiah's accession Jeremiah sought to dispel the view which had taken root in Judah that Jerusalem and the temple could never be destroyed (chs. 7 and 26). He recognized that though they may be adhering to the letter of the law found in the temple, probably Deuteronomy or part of it,[43] there had been no fundamental change of heart on the part of either leaders or people. To regard Jerusalem as a kind of lucky charm guaranteeing safety and security was a rejection of the authority and supremacy of God. Only the destruction of Jerusalem would teach them this.

In 605 the Babylonians defeated not only the Assyrians but also the Egyptians and from then on Judah fell into the hands of the Babylonians. Jehoiakim and many of his advisers looked for an opportunity to rebel, hoping that Egypt would help them. At this point Jeremiah can only advise them to remain loyal and subject to Babylon, advice which naturally came to be regarded as treason. This led to much of the persecution of Jeremiah which we have already described.[44] When Jerusalem was captured by Nebuchadnezzar in 597 Jeremiah persisted in this same message of submission when advising Zedekiah, the king whom Nebuchadnezzar had put on the throne. Torn for some time between the word of God through Jeremiah and the advice of his nobles Zedekiah finally took the advice of the latter and rebelled, with the result that city and temple were both destroyed in 587 B C. Still Jeremiah remained in Jerusalem, advising acceptance of the situation as the punishment of God until he was finally taken by friends to Egypt where he still continued to prophesy the success of the Babylonians, even against Egypt.

Zephaniah seems to condemn those practices which were prevalent either under Manasseh or before Josiah had reached an age or capacity to carry out reforms. Nahum is concerned wholly with the downfall of Nineveh the capital of Assyria which took place in 612. Habakkuk seems to see the Babylonians as a nation coming to punish Judah and so probably he was speaking as a contemporary of Jeremiah, between 609 and 600.

Ezekiel's ministry spans the period from about 592 to beyond 587. He had apparently been carried away captive in 597 by Nebuchadnezzar and, like Jeremiah, he sees the destruction of Jerusalem as inevitable, though he is speaking mainly to his fellow-exiles. After the city has fallen in 587 his message becomes one of hope and renewal because now Judah has been punished and the way is open for God to restore her. The hopes of renewal, after punishment, in the earlier prophets could now be fulfilled and God would gather his people to bring them back to their own land again.

The prophecies in Isaiah 40–55 come from a little later still. Here again it is the renewal of the Jews which fills the horizon. Punishment has been effected. For this prophet, however, a new historical situation is arising to make restoration possible. The Babylonian empire began to decline in power when Nebuchadnezzar died in c. 562 B C. His successors were weak and there was a new star on the horizon. A certain Cyrus, a Persian, was conquering in all directions and the prophet saw his activities as the God-given basis for the restoration of the Jews (Is. 44:28, 45:1ff.). His prophecies are therefore full of hope that the Jews will return to Zion, brought there by God just as surely as God had brought Moses and his people out of Egypt. This new event would form the basis of the future life of Judah just as the exodus had been its basis, for some at least, in days before the exile. Babylon fell to Cyrus in 538 and permission was given to the Jews, along with other captured peoples, to return to their homeland. Meanwhile, the people left in Judah throughout the fifty years of the exile were in a very poor state, with no leadership and few resources. The Edomites were constantly preying upon them from the south and the little book of Obadiah is a threat against the Edomites for so taking advantage of the weakness of Judah.

Although some Jews returned to Jerusalem and Judah in 538 many were content to stay behind in the relatively more comfortable conditions in Babylon. Those who did return soon found that conditions in Palestine robbed them of the ability to reconstruct the nation, its capital and its temple. Into this situation came Haggai and Zechariah, urging the people to rebuild the temple as a prelude to the prosperity for Judah which God would then grant. They seem to have envisaged the governor Zerubbabel as being the new leader of the state at first (Hagg. 2:10, Zech. 4:2-6, 6:9). Either that, or he and Joshua, the priest, ruling jointly.[45] As things turned out, however, from now on it was the high priest who was the effective ruler in Judah.

It is difficult to be certain about the date at which the prophecies in Malachi and Joel were spoken. They may have extended beyond 500 BC. But the compiler of the prophetic books points out at the very end of Malachi that this is the end of prophecy pending the coming of a new Elijah (Mal. 4:5).

Of course, the prophetic books do contain teaching which is not directly concerned with historical events and circumstances. But all that they say and do has to be seen in the first place against the background of these events. Only then may we go on to draw from them further lessons for our own faith or for our own times. We shall have more to say about this later.[46]

Finally, if we ask where the prophets proclaimed their messages the simple answer must be: wherever they could gather a crowd of people together to hear them. Amos apparently chose the sanctuary at Bethel. Isaiah addressed the people in Jerusalem and met king Ahaz 'by the conduit of the upper pool' wherever that may be (7:3).[47] No doubt he gave his advice to Hezekiah in the king's court. Jeremiah certainly spoke in the temple court (ch. 7), but also gave private advice to the king from prison or the guardroom. At the same time he performed his prophetic actions in various places in and around Jerusalem and finally prophesied in Egypt to those who were with him there. Ezekiel in Babylon could no longer use the temple courts or the king's court in Jerusalem. Instead he seems to have gathered the nobles and leaders in or near his own house (8:1). Thus there is no special 'prophet's corner'. Wherever men could be found who needed to hear the word of God the prophets were there to proclaim it, not in a vacuum, but in the context of the historical circumstances in which they and their people found themselves. Many of them foresaw and had to foretell the downfall of Samaria and Jerusalem interpreting the events in advance as the judgement of God upon his rebellious people. Others looked back on those same events and recognized the judgement as having been carried out and completed. Then they could turn again to the future that lay ahead for Judah if only she would be the people of God and, in obedience, act accordingly.

7. Shaping the Message

Anyone with an important message to communicate must be concerned with the 'form' in which he expresses himself. A sermon is different from a lecture, though sometimes the two may overlap. A political speech is different again while a 'call to the nation' in time of emergency will take yet another form. Within each kind of address we use certain well established forms. 'We must ...' or 'Let us ...' introduce the exhortation which is in frequent use in sermons or in calls to action. 'I quote ...' would be out of place in such addresses and clearly belongs to the lecture. 'The ... party want to do so-and-so, but if they do then ...' betrays the Aunt Sally technique of the political speech. 'Have you heard the one about ...' belongs not so much to public address as to private small talk and conversation. So oral communication tends to have set forms and this is true of prophecy. If we are not to misunderstand the prophet's words we need to recognize what form he is using and what effect this has on the meaning of the words. To take more modern examples again, 'Queen Anne's dead' means one thing if spoken in a history lesson and quite another if used in conversation or small talk. Or take a phrase like, 'I hate you'; its meaning will vary according to whether it is being used in the course of an argument – 'quarrel form' – or as a statement of fact – 'narrative form' – or in fun – 'teasing form'.

Perhaps the most important thing that can be said about the prophets in this respect is that they spoke in a kind of rhythmic speech which is best categorized as poetry. True, it is not poetry in the strictly formal sense in which we understand the term; it is not composed poetry with strict metre and it has no rhyme. Yet the form is poetic[48] and therefore to understand the message of the prophets properly we have to pay attention to the characteristics of poetry.[49] First of all poetry is not concerned with precision of meaning in the way that a philosophical treatise is. It seeks to present issues sharply in black and white rather than argue a case and allow for a grey area somewhere between the two. Consequently its language is often vivid and unrestrained, making much use of metaphor and vivid imagery of various kinds. Further it seeks a personal reaction from the reader or hearer, a response not only in terms of emotion but also in terms of action. All these factors have to be borne in mind when interpreting Hebrew prophecy.

To help to achieve these aims Hebrew poetry very often uses 'parallelism'.[50] By this is meant that the poet, or prophet, expresses what he wants to say in one line of speech and then reinforces it with another. The second line may simply repeat in a different way the idea of the first, the two lines being wholly synonymous.

> Israel does not know,
> my people does not understand. (Is. 1:3)

Alternatively the second may in some way extend the meaning of the first

> When Israel was a child, I loved him,
> and out of Egypt I called my son (Hos. 11:1)

Such parallelism is by no means always used, but when it is the form adds something almost indefinable to the saying. We may say it lends to it a greater intensity. Certainly to omit one member in translation is to reduce the impact of the saying.

Several 'forms' can be distinguished in the prophetic books. First there are songs. A good example of this may be found in Isaiah 5:1-7, which is a wedding song. During the wedding celebration period it was customary for the 'best man' or bridegroom's friend to convey messages between the bride and the groom. This, then, is a bridegroom's song sung by the best man. It is a song about a husbandman and his vineyard and these are frequently metaphors for bridegroom and bride. Towards the end of the poem the husbandman/bridegroom is identified with Yahweh and the vineyard/bride is identified with Israel. How telling this song would be. Perhaps Isaiah sang it at the time of the Feast of Ingathering when the grapes were gathered from the vine. His hearers would understand the first metaphor. They would recognize it as a song about a bridegroom who prepared his bride for love in every way possible and the bride who still, in spite of all, remained frigid. What they would not be prepared for would be the further meaning explained by the prophet in v. 7. That would soon turn their joyful appreciation into angry opposition. On top of that there is a fine example of word play in v. 7 which cannot adequately be brought out in translation. The words for 'justice' and 'bloodshed' are almost identical (*mišpaṭ* and *mišpaḥ*); so are the words for 'righteousness' and 'cry' (*ṣedakah* and *ṣeʿakah*). Some fine examples of mocking songs are also found in Isaiah 14:4ff. and Isaiah 47.

In the earlier days of Israel her struggles against the Canaanites and other surrounding peoples was regarded as a kind of holy war and certain phrases became 'war cries', to be used as Israel prepared for battle. The prophets sometimes use these, but with a somewhat different meaning. The war cries are used ironically, as if to say let Israel prepare for battle, but the victory will not be hers. Yahweh has decreed that defeat is certain. So Jeremiah 4:5, Hosea 5:8, 8:1. Let the trumpet call bring Israel together but this time for defeat.

Many of the prophetic sayings are borrowed from the sphere of worship. For instance Amos 4:4 begins with the invitation 'come!' We should imagine the prophet at the sanctuary at Bethel calling the people to worship as the priests or other members of the cultic staff used to do, 'Come to Bethel'. But then, with astonishing daring, he adds 'and transgress!' Seen like this there could be no more telling condemnation of the worship which was being offered at Bethel. Cf. also Amos 5:4. In the anonymous prophet of the exile similar forms are used more positively, as we might expect of one whose task is to promise restoration and not destruction. 'Sing to the LORD a new song' (Is. 42:10) reminds us at once of some of the psalms, especially Psalms 96 and 98. In worship sometimes lamentation was made about the circumstances in which the psalmist stood. Frequently these begin with 'How ...' or 'How long ...?' Examples of this form may be found in Isaiah 1:21, Amos 5:2f., Micah 1:8, 7:1ff., Jeremiah 8:18.

Again language from the law courts is also borrowed and used by the prophets, their prophecies being set out in the form of legal disputations. In Isaiah 3:13 Yahweh the judge is issuing his verdict against the elders and princes of his people, while in Hosea 12:2 he brings his indictment against Israel, the grounds on which he will punish her. Recognition of this form in Isaiah 1:18 helps to elucidate the meaning. Again Yahweh is the judge, but in this case he does not simply dispense judgement. Instead he invites the defendants to a discussion to see whether a way can be found to avoid punishing them. So he offers them the opportunity of forgiveness. Though their sins are like scarlet they may (better than 'shall' as in RSV) become white as snow, they may become like wool. Then in the following verses he sets out the options which are before the people, obedience or rebellion and their consequences.

From time to time the whole assembly of Israel met together. Deuteronomy gives us a picture of such a gathering in chapter 4 when the leader of the people 'calls upon heaven and earth to witness' against their behaviour (v. 26). In the same way the prophet can take up this form of speech and address Israel or Judah calling upon heaven and earth, that is, upon everything, to bear witness to the sin of the people (Is. 1:3, Jer. 6:19).

Already in chapter 4 we have mentioned the 'messenger formula' *This is what the Lord has said*, and its significance. Von Rad,[51] quoting Köhler's figures, says that the phrase occurs 14 times in Amos, 44 in Isaiah, 157 in Jeremiah, 125 in Ezekiel, once in Obadiah, Micah and Nahum, three times in Haggai and nine times in Zechariah. The only books in which it is not found are those of Hosea, Joel, Habakkuk and Zephaniah. So it can be seen how prevalent this form is. Sometimes, though by no means always, the message is closed by the phrase 'says Yahweh'. The form indicates the relationship which the prophet understood himself to have with Yahweh. He was his messenger entrusted with his word. Numbers 22:15f. illustrates exactly how this form was used. Balak the king of Moab sent his princes as messengers to Balaam. When they arrived they did not transpose Balak's words into reported speech but, beginning with the messenger formula, 'This is what Balak said', they went on to report the exact words he had spoken to them. So, as we have seen, the prophet's words, when introduced in this way, are the very words he believed Yahweh had spoken to him.

On many occasions the message introduced by the messenger formula begins with 'Therefore ...' and so becomes the second half of a larger unit of speech, the first part being the prophet's own assessment of the situation and the second the word of Yahweh which is now dropped like a stone into a pond, setting up ripples which will affect those to whom it is addressed. (Is. 1:21-26, Amos 1:1-3, Jer. 23:1-2, Mic. 2:1-3.) But this combination of a description of the situation by the prophet followed by a threat from Yahweh is often found without the messenger formula as well, the first part being introduced by 'Woe ...' and the second by 'therefore'. These two parts are known as the 'diatribe' and the 'threat' (Is. 5:11-13, Amos 6:4-7, Micah 2:1-3).[52] The form is not absolutely rigid and fixed but can be varied if the prophet so wishes. Sometimes there is no 'Woe' at the beginning of the diatribe (Is. 9:13). The threat may be introduced by a strong oath instead of 'therefore' (Is. 5:8-10) or by 'Behold ...' (Nahum 3:5) or by a simple 'because ...' (Hab. 2:6ff.). Nor should we be justified in thinking that if one part occurs without the other something has been lost from the text. Certainly the prophets used these various existing forms of speech, but they were not rigidly bound by them and we must always leave room for their own oratorical skill to modify and even break down the forms they use.

This analysis of forms is not simply a sterile academic exercise; it is an important tool for the understanding of the prophets' message. Once it is recognized that the message is in poetry or that it owes its form to various cultural and religious contexts, the danger of a too superficial interpretation is avoided. It involves a much deeper search for the meaning but this is rewarded by a fuller and more profound understanding of the prophets and their message.

8. Interpreting the Traditions

So long as the prophets were seen as the real founders of Israelite religion, preceding the formulation of the Law and the composition of the pentateuch, they could be regarded as innovators, men who brought new light and understanding about God and his dealings with men. They could be seen as people who laid great stress on social behaviour and ethics so that out of their teaching there developed the strict monotheism of later Judaism. Thus the prophets were given the highest place in Israelite religion as those who displaced the cult, the magic, the polytheism of the earlier days. Once it was realized that much in the pentateuch was very ancient and had been passed on orally for centuries this view could no longer be held in such a sharp form and it became clear that the prophets were not producing a new, higher religion out of the old one, but were using traditional material and ideas as the basis of their message.[53]

Traditions, for instance, about the jealous God, who would allow no rival alongside him so far as the Israelites were concerned, were picked up and reaffirmed by the prophets. Some traditions had become misunderstood and wrong conclusions drawn from them. These the prophets also took up but as they did so they re-interpreted them, throwing fresh light upon them, bringing new meaning out of them and making heavier demands on the people on the basis of them.[54] Yet other traditions about Israel's relationship with Yahweh were re-interpreted as being still in the future. We have already seen how the prophets' teaching is closely related to and concerned with contemporary events and circumstances; this is their historical background. To these circumstances they brought the 'word of God' and this was so often couched in terms of the ancient and well-known traditions which had become the basis of the life of the chosen people of God. It is to these traditions and to the use of them by the prophets that we now turn.

We begin with the election traditions. The two nations of Israel and Judah believed themselves to be the chosen people of God. The idea is prominent in the pentateuch and the historical writings. Abraham had been specially called and chosen by God, and his offspring were linked with him in this relationship with God (Gen. 12:1-3). In bringing his people out of Egypt under Moses God was again seen as choosing Israel (Exod. 19:5, Deut. 7:6ff.). Yet again God chose David and promised him a dynasty that would last for ever (2 Sam. 7). Consequently David's people were also chosen, sharing in some way the status of their king. There is little doubt that by the time we reach the prophetic period these traditions about Israel's election were being understood as a guarantee of her safety and security against all threats and dangers, irrespective of her conduct.

Amos now takes up these traditions and develops them in two ways. First he turns them against Israel. Election carries with it responsibilities in regard to behaviour and these Israel has failed to fulfil. Therefore, instead of protecting them and giving them prosperity because they are the chosen people, God will punish them for precisely the same reason. As his chosen people they ought to have known better and are therefore deserving of greater punishment (3:2). In chapter 9 he broadens the idea. Because of her sin Israel is now no longer in a privileged position. Even the Philistines and the Syrians had been in God's hands every bit as much as Israel and Israel's standing before God is now no different from theirs.

Hosea, too, sees these traditions as coming to an end. There is to be a separation of Israel from Yahweh comparable to that of Hosea from his adulterous wife (ch. 2). Israel has beccme thoroughly involved in Canaanite religious practices (2:8ff.) and so no longer 'knows' Yahweh (5:3ff.). This 'knowing' is more than an intellectual grasp; it is the familiarity which arises out of a close relationship and this is now over. There is no hope for the elect. The names of his children in chapter 1 indicate that Israel is to be 'not pitied' and 'not my people'. But then Hosea can take up this election tradition again and make it the basis of a new hope and a new relationship. Yahweh will begin afresh with Israel. She will have to go back to Egypt (9:3, 11:5) not literally, of course, but metaphorically. Then, because God's love extends beyond the separation as does Hosea's love for his unfaithful wife, God will call her anew (11:8). So the 'valley of Achor' where Israel had first sinned after entering the promised land (Josh. 7) will become a door of hope (2:14f.). Israel will respond to this new call and once again become 'my people' (2:23).

In the teaching of the southern prophet Isaiah these election traditions associated with the exodus from Egypt are scarcely found, if at all. The predominant tradition used by him is that of the election of Zion and its security. Psalms 46, 48 and 76 show that this was an established tradition, probably by the time of Isaiah, though it is exceedingly difficult to be sure about the date of psalms. On the one hand, however, the kings Ahaz and Hezekiah seem to have been reluctant to trust this tradition for both of them look to foreign nations for their help and security (chs. 7 and 31) and in face of their doubts Isaiah re-asserts that Yahweh alone will protect Jerusalem from her enemies (10:27–34, 17:12–14, 29:8, 30:27–33, 31:1–8). Alliances with other nations are thus a sin against Yahweh.

At the same time Isaiah can turn this tradition inside out, at least so far as the people of Judah is concerned, for the attack of the Assyrians which is part of the plan and purpose of God (10:5) is a 'strange work' – strange because it involves the defeat of the people chosen by God. But when Isaiah turns his eyes to the future that lies beyond the judgement of God Zion plays a prominent part in that future (2:1–5). It will be exalted as the centre of the world in the new age to come and all nations will make their way to it because this is the place from which God's law radiates its influence to all mankind. This choice of Zion, and consequently of Judah as a whole, is closely associated with the choice of David (2 Sam. 7). The tradition that God had chosen David and promised the continuance 'for ever' of the Davidic line was firmly held and this guaranteed and undergirded God's choice of Judah. If chapter 3 refers to Judah, as appears to be the case, then this tradition is called into question for Isaiah seems to foresee a time of anarchy when there will be no-one willing to take on the responsibility of ruling the land.

51

But again when he looks to the future his hope for the people's prosperity is guaranteed not by the accession of yet another 'son of David', for these had all proved faithless, but by the elevation by God of a 'new David', a 'shoot from the stump of Jesse' (11:1–5). The coronation of this new king is described in chapter 9 in terms familiar to the people from the coronation rites practised in Judah. The 'birth' of the 'son' is to be understood in exactly the same way as in Psalm 2, where the new king is adopted as the son of God and now stands in a filial relationship to him. His throne names in v. 6 indicate the power and wisdom by which he will rule. For the 'Israel' of the future security will again be guaranteed by the king, but this time by the rule of the ideal king who will always do what is right and will ensure that his people also do what is right (11:3–5). So Isaiah takes these election traditions associated with David and Zion, breaks them and then uses them again to describe the future which will once more involve an act of choice and calling by God.

Micah uses the same set of traditions, but for him, far from being the guarantee of Judah's safety, Jerusalem has become the focal point of Judah's sin (1:5). So both Samaria in the north and Jerusalem in the south will be devastated. Zion will become a 'ploughed field' and Jerusalem a 'heap of ruins' and the temple hill a 'wooded height' (3:12). In its present form the book again looks to the future and sees a new ruler emerging from Bethlehem (5:2), surely a new David. This new shepherd king will bring them prosperity and security in the way that the old tradition had promised.

For Habakkuk too the fact that God is using the Babylonians to destroy his chosen people is an astonishing and unbelievable thing for it conflicts with everything that tradition has asserted about God's protection of his own people (1:5ff.).

Some of the prophets use both Exodus and Zion election traditions side by side. Although Jeremiah is a Judaean his teaching is firmly based on the election traditions of the exodus. Part of the reason for this appears to be that he has been influenced by the work of Hosea and by the writings of Deuteronomy, both of which had their home in northern Israel. He takes up again Hosea's teaching that by her infidelity the chosen people, in this case Judah, had become a harlot (ch. 2) and the result of this must be a divorce between Yahweh and Judah (3:1–5). God is not bound to his people irrespective of their conduct and just because he has chosen them. He is free to cast them off and this he will do. The old covenant is abrogated (31:31). Yet God will begin anew and the covenant tradition is the means by which Jeremiah formulates his hope. Yahweh will make a new covenant which will not be like the old one. True, in some ways it is; the relationship between God and his people will be re-established, as in the first place, solely on God's initiative. But this time God's requirements will not be engraved on stone for it has proved impossible to fulfil these; they will be so engraved on people's wills that their will will become identical with God's will.[55]

Here indeed is a new twist to the tradition. At the same time there are one or two references to the Zion–David traditions. The belief that the temple could never be destroyed because it was the dwelling place of God is vigorously denied (ch. 7). That other symbol of the presence of God, the ark, now in the temple, had not guaranteed the security of Shiloh where it was housed, nor could the temple be regarded as a talisman protecting Jerusalem and Judah. Indeed the inviolable city must be destroyed (6:1ff., 8:19, 9:19, 14:19, 18:11). There are passages in the book which take up this tradition into its hopes for the future. The present Davidic dynasty is coming to an end. Jehoiakim, who is the 'signet ring on God's hand' (i.e. who bears the authority of God to rule) will be pulled off God's finger (i.e. will cease to rule as God's vice-gerent, 22:24–27). But afterwards God will 'raise up for David a righteous branch' and so provide them with a new king (23:5f., cf. 30:9) and Zion, too, will be restored (30:18, 31:12).

Ezekiel also uses the exodus traditions but in a rather unusual form. Chapter 20 sees the disobedience of the Hebrews as going right back to the time in Egypt itself and because of it God nearly left them there even though he had chosen them (v. 5). The whole tradition is one of rebellion and has to be set alongside chapter 16 which describes God's persistent and unfailing care, though this, too, ends in failure. Although in chapter 20 the end of the road of disobedience is left open it is almost certain that for Ezekiel the end of the road has now been reached and Israel's election is being abrogated. At the same time Jerusalem figures largely in his prophecies. Astonishingly Yahweh has left the temple and Jerusalem (ch. 10) and has himself become a sanctuary to the exiles (chs. 1 and 11:16). When he turns to the future there is little, if any, use of the exodus traditions to describe it. If any tradition predominates it is that of creation to which we shall turn later. But there is a picture in chapter 34 of Yahweh as the good shepherd, which is a title for the divine king, who will provide for Israel a new under-shepherd, David (34:23, cf. 37:24ff.). Again this is a fresh start which God makes with his people. Chapters 40–48 may or may not come from Ezekiel himself, but in any case the idea of a restored Jerusalem and an ideal temple are prominent in this vision of the future. In some respects the election themes are somewhat superseded by the frequent statements that both punishment and restoration are really motivated by God's concern for his own name, that is, his reputation in the world as a holy God. By his acts all nations will be able to recognize that he and he alone is God.

The prophet of Isaiah 40–55 also combines traditions in a quite remarkable way. Naturally enough, since he stands on the other side of the judgement of exile, there is little reference to the past. The old relationship between Yahweh and Israel was brought to an end by those two great catastrophes, the fall of Samaria and Jerusalem. Therefore the former things are no longer to be remembered because God is now about to do something new (43:18f.). This new thing is described in a surprising way. It is, of course, the return from Babylon to their own land, but it is described in language which recalls the exodus from Egypt. Indeed it is no exaggeration to call it a second exodus. Now, as then, it is an act of redemption; now, as then, it is to be brought about by God alone who is the redeemer (41:14 and often). They will again cross the desert (40:3) but this time its difficulties will be smoothed out by God and it will become fertile (41:19). Now, as then, Yahweh is a warrior God (42:13. cf. Exod. 15). Whether the waters of 43:2 are the metaphorical waters of trouble as often in the psalms or the waters of the Red Sea is uncertain, but there are clear references to the latter (50:2, 51:10f.).

But for all this emphasis on the language of the exodus the return is not, as in earlier tradition, to the promised land, Canaan, the land flowing with milk and honey. Rather the prophet here picks up the other tradition of election. The return is to Zion. Yet there is no reference to a new David as one might expect. The promises which were made to David are now extended to all (55:1–5). The only other possible reference to a new king is in the figure of the Servant in places like chapter 53. The Servant and his sufferings have been thought by some to show some similarity with the rituals associated with the kingship in Judah and therefore some regard him as a kingly figure.[56] Others, however, point to certain prophetic characteristics and regard him as a figure like Moses.[57] In either case the writer not only picks up the older traditions but transforms them into something new, for the Servant is something more than just a new king or a new prophet, a new David or a new Moses.[58]

Frequently the prophets mention the Day of Yahweh and it is clear that here also they are using a well-established tradition. Yet outside the prophetic books it is not easy to trace its origin. Some see its origin in the so-called holy war.[59] The great battles which Israel is said to have fought to establish herself in Canaan were won because this was Yahweh's doing and he was with them to give them victory. The Day of Yahweh, therefore, was the day of defeat for Israel's enemies and of exaltation of Israel over them. Others see the idea of the Day of Yahweh as developing with the cult.[60] On the enthronement of the earthly king Yahweh promised him victory and universal dominion (Ps. 2, 89:23). Further, there are psalms which speak of Yahweh's own kingship and look forward to his universal rule. This day of celebration may have become the Day of Yahweh and since each year this universal rule failed to materialize the idea of the Day was thrown into the future and the hope emerged of a future Day in which both Yahweh's and Israel's dominion over the world would become a reality. However the tradition arose we may be sure that it held a fond place in Israel's hopes for her future. Obadiah 15ff. expresses this hope clearly enough.

Amos tells us that the people of the Northern Kingdom were looking forward to the Day of Yahweh as a day of victory and light, the latter being a metaphor for salvation. But Amos shatters these hopes by declaring that the Day will be a day of utter darkness (5:18ff.). Israel will be judged in exactly the same way as the other nations and will share their fate. It may be that Hosea shares these views when he speaks in 1:5 of 'that day'. Certainly 'that day' is a day of judgement for Israel in Isaiah (7:18, 20, 21, 23) and in Micah (2:4, 3:5f.). But perhaps the strongest expression of all is in Zephaniah 1:14ff. where he describes it as a 'day of wrath'. Ezekiel (7:7–10,19 and Joel 1:15, 2:2) also take up the theme in the same way.

Yet this tradition, too, can be transformed by the prophets so that the original element of hope is restored. Once the day of wrath has come and gone a new Day of Yahweh will follow. Hosea can see 'that day' as a day in which Israel will call Yahweh not 'my baal', but 'my husband'. It is a day of new covenant and new peace when Israel's true relationship with Yahweh will be restored (2:16f., 20). The book of Isaiah contains similar hopes (4:2, 11:10, 11:11) though these passages are often regarded as later interpretations of Isaiah's original message. Ezekiel (38:19f.) and Micah (7:11, 12) use the phrase similarly. But far more often references to the future are introduced by phrases such as 'in those days' or 'in days to come' and here it seems that these are independent of the tradition of the Day of Yahweh.

The prophetic condemnation of social abuses is to be seen against the background of the Law though it is usually hard to decide which particular collection of law underlies any prophetic teaching. Hosea 4:2 with its reference to swearing, lying, killing, stealing, committing adultery and murder seems dependent on the Ten Commandments (Exod. 20:1–17) and it may be that Amos is concerned about breaches of the law as found in Exodus 21–23.[61] References to the maltreatment of widows, orphans and aliens are frequent but regulations concerning these are found in many of the law codes. The real sin, however, is not so much the breaking of a written law as the failure to maintain a relationship with God which would make such breaches unthinkable. The passage referred to from

Hosea (4:2) is preceded by the statement that they lack knowledge of God, that is, their personal relationship with him is broken and failure to keep the law is simply the consequence of this. Nevertheless the prophets' condemnation of unjust judges and their pleas for a proper execution of justice show that they uphold the law whether this is understood as a codified collection or, more simply, as the instructions of Yahweh (Is. 1:23, Jer. 5:28, Ezek. 5:6f., Hos. 4:2, Amos 5:7,15, Mic. 3:9–11, Zech. 7:9, Mal. 4:4).

So in Isaiah's vision of the future (2:1–5) the law will go out again from Zion and all nations will come to learn it. For Jeremiah, however, the law has become inadequate. Judah's failure is simply that she has been totally unable to keep it. Therefore, in his view of the future (31:31ff.) there is no point in God simply providing a new law, even an internal one, for the people will be just as incapable of keeping that. What he envisages, then, is a law written, engraved upon the heart and by this he means not merely an internalized law but rather that the very will and intention of the people will be made to conform to the will of Yahweh.[62] Ezekiel expresses this same hope even more clearly when he says that God will give the restored people 'a new heart', that is, a new understanding of what God wants and a new will to do it (36:26f.).

We have already mentioned the tradition of the holy war. This is now sometimes called the 'Yahweh War' because one part of the tradition is that everything depends on Yahweh and Israel's part in the exodus and occupation was purely passive. Examples of this are found in Exodus 14:13f. where Israel, at the Sea, has only to stand still and wait for Yahweh to act, and in Judges 7 where Gideon must reduce his forces by choosing those who were least watchful so that Israel would not be able to claim any part in the victory. This latter event is specifically referred to in Isaiah 9:4. It is Isaiah more than any other prophet who uses this tradition. All through his ministry he insisted on the need to rely on Yahweh alone, to leave matters with him. The people must not take matters into their own hands nor seek help from foreign alliances. So, facing Ahaz in 735 BC, he calls on him to 'be quiet' and, with nice play on words, threatens 'If you will not believe (ta'aminu), surely you shall not be established (te'amenu)'.

57

Later, to Hezekiah and the Judaeans of his day he affirms that 'in quietness and trust shall be your strength' (30:15) and therefore trust in the Egyptians is completely misplaced (31:1ff.).

Associated with this in Exodus 14:13 is the 'work of Yahweh' which he will do on Israel's behalf. This Isaiah again stands on its head; his work will be 'strange and alien' for he will fight against Jerusalem (28:21). It may be this same 'trust' tradition which also leads Hosea to condemn foreign alliances (7:11). Perhaps, too, it underlies the prophecies of Isaiah 40–55 where the Jews do nothing, but the return is planned solely by Yahweh who raised up Cyrus the Persian (44:28, 45:1), who would level off the hills and valleys (40:2), who would return at the head of his people and feed his flock (40:11).

Finally there is the traditional view of Yahweh as creator which is already found in the early account of Genesis 2:4ff., written down before 900 B C, and is used widely in the psalms (e.g. Ps. 8:3,6, 19:1, 90:17) and especially in Psalms 93, 95–99.[63] It is true that these latter psalms are sometimes thought to come from the post-exilic period,[64] but more likely they are pre-exilic and in any case there is plenty of evidence that for pre-exilic Israel it is Yahweh and not Baal who controls the world and therefore presumably it was thought that he also created it. Though this tradition does not have a major place in the teaching of the pre-exilic prophets Amos does contain three 'doxologies' which speak of Yahweh as creator (4:13, 5:8, 9:5).

During the exile there is ample evidence that this tradition came into greater prominence. The opening chapter of Genesis comes from this period and it is in the prophecies of Isaiah 40–55 that we find most use made of it (40:21–31, 42:5, 43:1 etc.). One of the most interesting features of his use of it is the way in which he combines it with the traditions of the exodus, and particularly the second exodus, to which we have already referred. This combination was made more possible by the fact that creation could always be seen as redemption from Chaos and that the redemption from Egypt led to the creation of the people of God. Further, the creation tradition made use of the idea of the sea which was overcome at creation while, of course, the Red Sea played a prominent part in the exodus tradition. So in Isaiah 51:9–11 these ideas are brought together. 'Rahab' and the 'dragon' are both used of chaos in the Babylonian mythology, but Rahab had also become a nickname for Egypt. The drying up of the sea may refer either to the creation of dry land or to the separation of the waters of the Red Sea, but by the second half of v. 10 he is clearly thinking in terms of the exodus. This ability to take up traditions and mingle them is a feature of this prophet. Naturally the emphasis on Yahweh as the sole creator leads to the logical conclusion that there is no god besides him anywhere in earth or heaven. Monotheism, then, is clearly and unambiguously expressed (45:5 etc., etc.).

In these ways the prophets took up existing traditions and used them in their preaching, sometimes re-affirming them, sometimes turning them inside out, sometimes restoring them as descriptions of the future, sometimes modifying and re-interpreting them. In this way they reveal startling new insights into the purpose of God for his people and for his world.

9. The Fate of the Prophets' Words

What happened to the prophets' words once they had spoken them? We have seen that the prophets were really preachers, men whose weapon was the spoken word. But what happened when, for instance, Amos left Bethel and, as we presume, returned to his work in Tekoa? How were his spoken words preserved and by whom? It is possible, of course, that the prophets themselves committed their spoken words to writing after they had spoken them. But this is unlikely, not because the prophets were necessarily incapable of writing, but because the books as we now possess them show evidence of a lengthy process of transmission and compilation. But, if not the prophets themselves, then who? Scarcely the religious or court officials whom the prophets attacked for they would have no interest in preserving the words they despised. Scarcely the rank and file of the Israelites, who either ignored or rejected their teaching. They had no official secretaries, so who then? The usual answer has been that it was their disciples who wished to preserve their teaching for future generations, but when we turn to the Old Testament to find evidence of these disciples we find that they are strangely elusive.[65]

In the historical books and in Amos 7:14 we have mention of the 'sons of the prophets' or 'prophetic guilds', as they are sometimes called. Frequently, however, the classical prophets are seen to be in opposition to these. In 2 Kings 4:1, 38ff., 6:14 Elisha seems to be on good terms with them and may even be a leader among them. But already in 1 Kings 22 Micaiah has a different message from them and has to oppose them. Amos 7:14 has been the subject of a great deal of study and different views of it have emerged.[66] It is most likely, however, that Amaziah placed Amos in the same category as the 'sons of the prophets', to which the prophet replies that he is not one of them and that his own prophecies are independent of them. It is hardly likely that we shall find disciples among these.

A crucial text in this regard is found in Isaiah 8:16. The RSV, in fact, uses the word 'disciple' in its translation. The difficulty can be seen as soon as we compare the NEB which has 'Fasten up my message, seal the oracle with my teaching' and yet offers as an alternative in the margin 'among my disciples'. The word in question is an adjective meaning 'taught' and either a person or a thing can be taught. So it may mean either 'disciples' or 'teaching'. In support of the former may be the fact that in v. 18 Isaiah refers to himself and the 'children (sons) whom the Lord has given him' as 'signs and portents in Israel'.[67] The phrase 'sons of the prophets' often does refer to the group of prophets and 'sons' may here suggest such a group of followers of Isaiah.

At the same time, however, it is more likely that the word 'children' is to be taken literally for Isaiah's two sons, Shear-jashub and Maher-shalal-hash-baz, both stand before the people, along with the prophet, as signs set before the king and the people (7:3 and 8:1–4). His message is bound up in the names of these children so that even when Isaiah is silent the very sight of his children with their special names would recall the prophet's message. So the uncertainty about the meaning of this text means that it would be dangerous to use it as evidence for the presence of disciples unless it could be supported by evidence from elsewhere.

Such support has been sought in Amos 7:10 where Amos is said to conspire against Jeroboam.[68] The argument is that you cannot 'conspire' with yourself; the word always implies other people with whom you conspire. This is certainly the case in 1 Samuel 22:8, 13, 2 Kings 15:10. But in 1 Kings 15:27 and 16:9 the word is used again where only one person is concerned and this is particularly the case in 2 Kings 10:9. The argument is really faulty because the Hebrew word may not have quite the same range of meaning as the English equivalent which has to be used in translation. The words 'to plot' and 'to conspire' may both be used to translate the Hebrew word. The former can be done alone, the latter involves more than one person.

The call to 'hear, and testify against the house of Jacob' in Amos 3:13 is addressed to more than one person since the verbs are in the plural. To whom are the words addressed if not to Amos and his disciples?[69] Here, however, it may be the form used which demands plural verbs. This address is cast in the form in which the leader of an assembly calls upon witnesses, sometimes heaven and earth. The grammar is thus determined by the form and no firm conclusions about disciples can be gained from this.

With Jeremiah we seem to be in somewhat better case for chapter 36 tells how Jeremiah dictated some of his prophecies to Baruch. Though Baruch is simply referred to as a scribe and not a disciple, he does become involved in the proclamation of the prophecy since when Jeremiah could no longer go to the temple to speak for himself Baruch went and read the prophecies for him. When Baruch became disheartened by the prophecies of doom which he, along with Jeremiah, had to proclaim Jeremiah had to teach him that the acceptance of this message was necessary and Baruch must be content if he was allowed to live at all (Jer. 45). Whether or not he is described as a disciple he certainly looks like one. Yet, as we shall see later, there was a good deal more editorial work done on the teaching of Jeremiah in addition to the work of Baruch which was in the main simply transcription.

Finally there is a reference to 'those who are taught' in Isaiah 50:4.[70] This is somewhat obscured by the NEB which has 'teacher' at this point, though it is difficult to see how the word can mean that. The context suggests that the prophet is claiming for himself the tongue of such people as are taught by God, and whose words therefore can be relied upon. But then there is no reference here either to disciples or the prophets.

Indeed the evidence for such disciples is extremely slight. The prophets, as far as we can see, were lone figures who lacked the support of people who accepted their teaching and then helped in the promulgation of it. And yet, how else can their words have been preserved? We are bound to say that however slight the evidence may be there must have been some people who listened and who realized that their words had the ring of truth and authority about them and so preserved them for the future so that they may be used and re-used later by others. Beyond that we cannot go at the present time.

It has been suggested that their words were passed on in more than one circle of followers,[71] or 'traditionists' as they are often called. The evidence for this comes from the books themselves which sometimes contain the same oracle twice or two accounts of the same event. Jeremiah 21:8-10 is repeated almost word for word in 38:2-3, while the account of Jeremiah's preaching in the courts of the temple in chapter 7 is repeated in chapter 26. In the former stress is laid upon the sermon itself; in the latter it is the outcome of the preaching which occupies the writer. In the same way it is possible that Hosea 1, which is biographical, and Hosea 3, which is autobiographical, are two accounts of the same experience of the prophet which have been preserved in two different circles and which were both included by the final editors of the book. Of course, where an oracle is repeated it could be argued that the prophet spoke the same words on more than one occasion, and that is likely enough since it is the word of God which, by repeating it, he is speeding on its way towards fulfilment. All the same, the presence of different accounts of the same event does seem to point to a process of compilation which is somewhat complex and which we cannot now describe in any detail or with any certainty. The most we can say is that the process began with the oral material which was collected and written down later.

It has long been recognized that the books as we now have them contain words which were not spoken by the prophet concerned, but which are 'additions to the text'. Such a phrase presupposes that after the prophecies were written down someone wilfully interfered with the writing and added words of their own to it. In some places it may be that the prophet's own words were too frightening to contemplate and were therefore softened by the addition of some words of hope or promise. The book of Amos paints such a picture of the end of the Northern Kingdom of Israel and therefore, it is suggested, a later editor added the final section in chapter 9:8-15 in order to take the edge off the harsh message of judgement. In the same way the passages of hope in Isaiah 2:2-4, 4:2-6,

9:2-7 and 11:1-9 have been regarded as hopeful additions by later editors to the words of Isaiah, particularly as the words in Isaiah 2:2-4 are found also in Micah 4:1-4, fulfilling a similar purpose.

But once it is realized that the words of the prophet were preserved first orally and then in written form by people who were concerned not only for their preservation but also for their continued proclamation in new circumstances, in other words, by people who used the prophets' words as the basis for their own preaching and applied them to their own day, we begin to see that these 'additions' are not thoughtless insertions, but are the result of the interpretation of the prophetic word. Consequently the prophetic books contain not only the words of the prophet but also the interpretation of those words by others in a later period.

Amos' teaching was, as we have seen, related to the circumstances prevailing in the Northern Kingdom of Israel towards the end of the reign of Jeroboam II, about 750 BC. But his teaching was remembered and preserved by others and became known in the Southern Kingdom of Judah. Consequently what he had said about Israel could now be applied also to Judah by later prophetic preachers.[72] So Judah was now included in the list of nations who had sinned (2:4-5). This is how Amos might have spoken about Judah if he had been alive and active, say, a hundred years later. But in Judah, unlike Israel, there was the tradition of the continuance of the Davidic line, to which we have already referred. Therefore though Amos' words of judgement were applicable to Judah it was necessary, in using them, to leave room for this belief. And so the final verses which refer to the 'Booth of David' being raised up are a part of this later preaching when Amos' words are being interpreted as relevant to Judah.

That earlier prophets' words could be taken up and re-interpreted in this way is shown clearly by the way in which Jeremiah 26:18f. picked up the unfulfilled prophecy of Micah 3:12 about the downfall of Jerusalem which had been spoken a hundred years before and applied it to his own day. Similarly, the language of Isaiah 4 shows this chapter to have been written at some time during the exile but it has to be seen not so much as an insertion into the book as an example of the way in which the prophecies of Isaiah were interpreted and used as texts for later preaching.

So the concern today is not simply to get back to the actual words of the prophet himself and to ignore these so-called 'additions'. Rather we should ask, 'What did the prophet himself say?' and then go on from there to ask, 'What did the later interpreters make of their words and how did they use them?' Then we ourselves may take our place in the line of interpreters which already had its beginning within the period during which the prophetic books were compiled.

There still remains the question as to whether we can identify these interpreters any more closely, for we have seen how hard it is to find evidence of any disciples. One answer which is being given nowadays is that the interpreters were often the Deuteronomists. This term is used to denote those who composed the book of Deuteronomy and those who continued to promulgate its teaching during the ensuing years down into the exilic period. The most common view is that Deuteronomy itself, or at least chapters 12–26 were written towards the end of the 8th century in the north, some time soon after the fall of the Northern Kingdom in 722 BC. Somehow or other it found its way into the south and was hidden in the temple during the reign of Manasseh. It was found there by Josiah's workmen in 621 BC and became the basis for his reforms. The writing of the book and its preservation was not due to one man but to a group or 'school', some think of Levites,[73] others of prophets.[74]

This Deuteronomic 'school' became active from now on, not only preaching the maxims of Deuteronomy but also compiling a history of Israel and Judah. Here they used old traditions about the past which they put together in such a way as to illustrate their basic beliefs that obedience to God brings prosperity and disobedience brings adversity. They were responsible for the Deuteronomic history, Joshua to 2 Kings.[75] Their selection of material for inclusion and their assessment of the reigns of the kings is always undertaken from this point of view. Yahweh had made a covenant with his people and adherences to the terms of this covenant brought blessing, whereas if the people turned away from the covenant they must expect to be cursed.

Interpretative passages in the prophetic books have been examined from this point of view and a strong consistency with Deuteronomic teaching has been noticed.[76] The passage already mentioned in Amos 2:4-5 is a good example of this. Again if we look at the prose sections in the book of Jeremiah these also show much evidence of the ideas and language of Deuteronomy and this makes it very likely that it was the school of Deuteronomists who collected the oracles and put the book into its present shape. This may well apply to the other prophetic books as well. The Deuteronomist historian of Joshua to 2 Kings hardly mentions the prophets at all and this rather strange fact could be explained if the same school was at the same time collecting together a companion volume of prophetic writings.

Attractive as this view may be we still cannot be sure that this is the correct explanation of things. It is easy to fall into the trap of attributing too much to the Deuteronomists and of thinking that the ideas they held and the language in which they expressed those ideas were unique to them, when this may not necessarily be the case.

There is, therefore, a fair amount of uncertainty about the way in which the words of the prophets found their way into books such as those we now find in the Old Testament. What we can say is that interpreters of the prophets can no longer be concerned only with what the prophets themselves actually said; they have to be equally concerned with the ways in which their words were interpreted and what they came to mean for those who followed them.

10. From Spoken Word to Written Book

Though we may speculate that a collection of prophetic books was made as early as the period of the exile we have no firm evidence for such a collection until getting on for four hundred years later. The Jewish historian Josephus, writing in the 1st century A D tells us that the prophetic age came to an end in the time of Artaxerxes I (465–424)[77] and in this he seems to be nearly enough correct. But when he says that the collection of the books was complete in the same period he is probably allowing his theories to distort the facts. Similarly in a late Jewish writing known as 2 Esdras (14:18-28) we are told that the whole of the Old Testament was dictated by Ezra to five men in forty days! This would also mean that the collection of prophetic books was complete during the 5th century, but here again the writer is allowing his belief that Ezra is the father of Judaism to influence his understanding of how the Old Testament came into being.

Rather more solid evidence comes from about 190 B C when a man called Sirach mentioned in his writings Isaiah, Jeremiah, Ezekiel and the Twelve Prophets (Wisdom of Sirach, 48:22–49:12). His grandson who wrote a prologue to the work about 117 B C said that his grandfather had studied 'the law, the prophets and the other books of the fathers'. Though we cannot be certain that this prophetic collection is identical with the prophetic books in our present Old Testament it is quite clear that there was such a collection in being by that time. All we can say, then, is that the process may have begun during the exile and was certainly completed, near enough, by the beginning of the 2nd century B C.

Earlier still the prophecies had been written down. Isaiah had apparently written some of his words so that they may stand as a witness to what he had said when he was no longer in a position to speak (Is. 30:8). We are told that this was the case with Jeremiah who dictated some of his words to Baruch when he was debarred from entering the temple (Jer. 36). Some of Ezekiel's prophecies are dated closely and give the impression of having been written soon after they were spoken. In addition we have to assume that other sympathizers, having heard the prophecies, felt it necessary to write them down so that the word of God may continue its course. Then, perhaps the Deuteronomists and others began to collect the prophecies and arrange them in books and into a prophetic collection.

The process is difficult to describe in detail but there are indications of it in the book of Isaiah and we may look at this book to illustrate the way in which the spoken word became a written book. Not everyone would agree with the analysis that follows but at any rate it is one possible analysis which shows the kind of things that must have happened.[78]

The book of Isaiah is divided into three main sections, chapters 1–39, 40–55 and 56–66. We shall be chiefly concerned with chapters 1–39 here. These thirty-nine chapters may, in turn, be divided into five sections. The first of these is chapters 2–12, which may be subdivided again into chapters 2–4, 5:1–30 + 9:8–11:16 and 6:1–9:7. Chapters 2–4 consist of a poem with a recurring refrain. It has a number of stanzas all threatening judgement (2:8–21), a series of threats against the rulers and leaders of the people whose sin will lead to anarchy (3:1-15) and a series of threats against the women folk, probably the wives of the above leaders, who encourage their husbands to sin (3:16–4:1). All these threatening passages are enclosed within two passages of hope, the first of which (2:1-4) is virtually identical with Micah 4:1-4 and the second of which (4:2-6) bears all the marks of exilic authorship. Thus we have a series of oracles which are almost certainly from Isaiah himself framed between two others, one of which may be from Isaiah and the other almost certainly not. Here we can see the hand of the collector at work arranging the teaching of the prophet.

Chapters 5:1–30 and 9:8–11:16 begin with the famous song of the vineyard which is sometimes thought to be one of the earliest utterances of Isaiah (5:1-7). It is followed by a collection of 'woes', chiefly against the leadership (5:8-24). Then there is another poem, 'The Outstretched Hand', which has four complete stanzas and refrains in 9:8-10:4, a fifth refrain in 5:25 the preceding stanza of which is missing, and finally a sixth stanza in 5:26-30 which has no refrain because the punishment is regarded this time as final. The order of the poem has been disturbed by the insertion of 6:1-9:7. The section concludes with an oracle of hope which could have come from Isaiah (11:1-7) but to this there has been added an extension (11:10-16) which comes from the exilic period.

Chapters 6:1-9:7 are a series of reports or memoirs, chapters 6 and 8 being autobiographical, chapter 7 biographical. All of these chapters are set firmly in the context of the threat to Judah by Israel and Syria in 735 BC. There is the account of the meeting of Isaiah and his son with Ahaz followed by a threat of Assyrian attack (ch. 7), the careful inscription of the name of another son which promises the withdrawal of the alliance of Israel and Syria with repeated warnings against appealing to Assyria for help instead of relying on the prophet's word which is God's word (ch. 8). These two chapters are set within the framework of Isaiah's call (ch. 6) and another oracle of hope (9:1-7). Here then is another small topical collection.

These three sections were probably collected together and a hymn of thanksgiving added to round off this larger collection. Its similarity with the psalms has led some to think that the collection may have been shaped within the cult, the worshipping life of Judah.

We may then turn to chapters 28–35, a collection of oracles which can nearly all be dated in 701 BC when the Assyrians were threatening Judah. This begins with a threat against the Northern Kingdom of Israel which acts as a kind of text for the rest against Judah (28:1-4). In the body of this section oracles of threat and warning alternate with oracles of hope (28:5–32:20). This is then provided with a liturgical appendix (33) and a conclusion which is similar in character to chapters 40–55 (34–35).

Another large collection is found in chapters 13–23. These are mostly oracles against foreign nations, but are interspersed with oracles concerning Judah. Such collections appear in all the major prophetic books and it is not clear which are from the prophet himself and which are provided by the collector or editor. There is a parody on 'The Outstretched Hand' (14:24-27) which almost certainly comes from a later hand than Isaiah's.

Chapters 24–27 are written in a style which is generally thought to be much later than Isaiah. Because of its content and style it is sometimes known as the 'little apocalypse'. It could have been used as a conclusion to chapters 13–23 or as an introduction to chapters 28–35. At any rate it forms a bridge between the two.

These four sections were then put together and provided with an introduction which is a kind of 'sampler' of Isaiah's teaching (ch. 1) and a historical conclusion (chs. 36–39). Thus we may account for the growth of Isaiah 1–39.

Later, during the exile another prophet uttered oracles promising the return to Zion. Possibly there are two smaller collections within chapters 40–55 (40–48 and 49–55), but there is no suggestion of different authorship here. It is simply that the subject matter is slightly different. Almost all scholars think this prophet lived during the exile and that these words were not spoken by Isaiah of Jerusalem.[79] Yet there is enough similarity of outlook and language to suggest that this later prophet was already familiar with the teaching of Isaiah and may have been a spiritual descendant of his. The similarity was strong enough for it to be included on the same scroll as the prophecies of Isaiah.

Chapters 56–66 are a catena of sayings which again are dependent on the earlier prophets and may have come from this same 'school' as they continued preaching in succession to Isaiah. There was room on the scroll also for those oracles and so they were placed after 40–55. The resulting scroll is then of roughly equal length with those of Jeremiah, Ezekiel and the Twelve. By the time the book was copied by the men of Qumran in the 2nd century BC the book was in this extended form, for their copy contains all sixty-six chapters, though there is a small space left after chapter 34 which may indicate that they thought of a different authorship from then on.

Now it has to be admitted that this account of the compilation and editing of the book is speculative. It is based largely on internal evidence, that is, what can be found within the book itself. There are other possible explanations, but whichever one is correct in detail we have to assume a long and complicated process such as is described here and, as has been said previously, the modern interpreter has to be concerned not only with the actual words spoken by Isaiah or the later prophets in the book, but with the beliefs of those who later used his prophecies as the basis for their own teaching and who collected them together, as far as these can be discerned.

III

The Prophets and their Religious Contemporaries

11. Criticism and Condemnation of Worship

We turn now to consider the relationship of the prophets to the religious establishment of their day and to ask what was their attitude to the worship being offered and to the whole 'cult' in all its forms. Did they show a radical opposition to the cult in itself or was it simply that they demanded different attitudes on the part of the worshippers? The answer to these questions is not easy; it depends upon the interpretation of several passages in the prophetic books which have been differently understood by scholars. It is important to come to these passages with an open mind and to examine them as carefully as possible.

Beyond all doubt there is a considerable amount of condemnation of both idolatry and syncretism. Where the people had turned away from Yahweh to worship idols or the gods represented by idols the prophets were not slow to condemn this apostasy. Some of the clearest references to idolatry are found in Isaiah 40–55 where the prophet warns against it by subjecting it to ridicule. How foolish it is to take a piece of wood, to use half of it to make a fire to warm oneself and then make of the other half an idol to worship (44:9-10)! Foreign gods are no better than the idols which may represent them. The Babylonian gods, Bel and Nebo, have to be carried in procession, whereas Yahweh has carried his people (46:1-4). Habakkuk also scorns the home-made idol which is utterly lifeless (2:18-19).

Syncretism is rather different. This involves the confusion of Yahweh with other gods and the introduction of practices into the worship of Yahweh which are wholly alien to him. Given the polytheism of Canaanite religion in which fertility of the earth is due in some measure to the sexual activities of the deities, then imitative sexual practices in worship may be understandable. But to introduce these same practices into worship of Yahweh is totally wrong because he is a different kind of God, the only god, who therefore has no female consort. It is to misunderstand Yahweh and to treat him as though he were Baal. Therefore cultic prostitution is condemned outright (Amos 2:7b, Hosea 4:14). They have failed to differenꞇiate between Baal, whom the Canaanites regarded as the giver of fertility to the land, and Yahweh who alone provides the corn and oil (Hosea 2:8). To consult mediums and wizards is not necessarily idolatrous but it introduces into the worship of Yahweh alien elements which deny the sole supremacy of Yahweh (Is. 8:10). So far, then, all is clear. The prophets wholly condemn worship which is offered to gods other than Yahweh and worship in which the unique character of Yahweh has been compromised.

But there are passages which show a very positive attitude to the cult and perhaps the most noticeable of these is in the call of Isaiah described in Isaiah 6. It really makes no difference whether we think of this as a real experience within the temple or as a vision using temple imagery. The confrontation by Yahweh, the awareness of sin, the experience of cleansing, the conviction of a call are all set firmly within a cultic context and this will not allow us to think that the prophet is opposed to the cult in itself. Further, in many prophetic passages concerning the future a renewed and purified cult plays a part (Jer. 17:26, Ezek. 40–48, Nahum 1:15, Hagg. 2:6ff., Zech. 4:8ff. etc.). In contrast to these, however, Hosea seems to see a future in which neither cult nor monarchy have any place because these are the very two things which have led Israel astray in the past. It may be that the phrase 'for many days' implies that this is a temporary arrangement until Israel shall have proved herself to be loyal. She must return to the wilderness (2:14) before she can regain her status before God. This implies that Hosea thought that there was no cult in the wilderness period, or, at any rate, they were without a cult which was in danger of becoming 'Baalised' and to this point we shall return in a moment.

Alongside this positive attitude to the cult we have to set the frequent demand for proper behaviour. The prophets certainly regarded the whole paraphernalia of worship as ineffective, and worse than that, even sinful unless it was accompanied by the kind of life which Yahweh required of them or at least by the intention to live that kind of life. In Isaiah 29:13f. the people 'draw near' to God, that is to say, they come into the presence of the divine king, with expressions of loyalty, but their wills are in no way conformed to his and what they do they do simply in conformity with custom and habit. According to Jeremiah 11:15f. Israel has no right to be in the temple when her deeds are vile and the sacrifices which she offers there will have no effect. Malachi would rather see the temple closed altogether than people offering sacrifices which were against the commands of God, being forbidden by law (1:6ff.).

It may be that a similar point is being made in Hosea 6:6 though this text begins to raise questions of interpretation. It runs,

> For I desire steadfast love and not sacrifice,
> the knowledge of God, rather than burnt offerings.

Now the lines are not strictly parallel though they are surely intended to be. The first line suggests that God wants one thing and not another; the second that he prefers one thing to the other. Should the preference expressed in the second line also determine the meaning of the first? Or should the word translated 'rather than' in the second line be translated 'without' in conformity with the first line? A similar ambiguity runs through a number of other passages and no decision about their meaning can be taken until they have been examined in the light of what we have already said.[80]

There is the ironic invitation of Amos to the people recorded in 4:4f. where their worship is nothing less than an act of rebellion against Yahweh. It is not clear whether Amos is charging the people with offering the correct number of sacrifices or whether he is saying that they offer more than the number required, but this makes no difference to his staggering statement that their worship is a sin. Unfortunately he does not say why it is a sin. It may be because, being a Judaean, he regards the cult at Bethel as schismatic and is therefore critical of their love to perform it 'so', that is, in

Bethel. Or it could be that the cult itself is condemned. They have come to love the cult instead of loving moral uprightness. They ought to 'love justice' (5:15) and this is what God requires of them, not sacrifice. Again it could be that the cult is condemned because it has come to have the place in their lives which should belong to Yahweh. The view has taken root that forgiveness is to be gained through performance of the cult whereas, according to Amos, it is the personal God who responds to man's repentance in forgiveness. If this is the case then it is a matter of priorities. Sacrifices are God-given vehicles for his forgiveness, but it is always God who forgives. There is no automatic, guaranteed forgiveness simply through the performance of certain acts, even when those acts are the means used by God to convey his forgiveness.

Whichever view is taken of 4:4f. Amos makes it clear that the worship at Bethel, Gilgal and Beersheba is useless and these very shrines will be destroyed because of Israel's sin (5:5f.), for justice is lacking in Israel. The strongest expression of condemnation of the cult is to be found in chapter 5:21f. Here God positively hates their worship and refuses their sacrifices. The great pilgrim feasts, the sacrifices, music and singing will all be taken away. In their place justice and righteousness are required by God, that is, behaviour which recognizes one's obligations to fellow Israelites on account of what God has done for the whole community. This looks like a condemnation of insincere worship again, worship without the accompanying moral qualities which God requires. Perhaps also there is a hint that they regard them as *their* feasts and forget that they are really *God's* feasts which have no meaning and no validity apart from God.

There is one other passage in Amos, a passage which is in prose and not in poetry and which must be regarded therefore as a separate oracle. It follows on in 5:25 from the previous passage just discussed. The implication of this verse is that sacrifice is no longer to be offered because it was not offered in the wilderness. The questions about this clearly expect the answer 'No, no sacrifice was offered then.' This raises the whole question of whether sacrifices were offered in the wilderness or not. We have already seen how Hosea suggested they were not.

Yet the biblical traditions preserved in the pentateuch do speak of a number of sacrifices offered by the Israelites in that period. Certainly Passover is located there, but since this was essentially a family festival it may have been regarded differently from the pilgrim feasts at the sanctuaries and as giving no authority for these. In Exodus 18:12 Jethro is said to have offered sacrifice followed by a cultic meal which he shared with Aaron, but not, apparently, with Moses! This is rather strange and may suggest that we are dealing here with a late tradition which sought to validate the Aaronic priesthood. At the Covenant ceremony on Mount Sinai described in Exodus 24:5-8 sacrifice is offered. Yet the important thing in the narrative is not the sacrifice but the use of the blood of the oxen for sealing the covenant and it may be that the account of sacrifice is a later amplification of the use of the blood in line with later cultic practice in ceremonies of covenant renewal. In any case some scholars think that the whole Sinai tradition was unknown to the prophets![81] For the rest it depends whether we see the whole legal corpus in Leviticus as being Mosaic, for Leviticus 1–9 certainly provides regulations for elaborate sacrifice and as it now stands this applies to the wilderness period. However, these chapters are most commonly regarded as coming from the exilic or post-exilic period in which case they would be unknown to the prophets.

So Amos' claim may be an accurate and justified one, that in pre-Canaanite days there was no sacrificial system among the Israelites associated with community feasts and that these entered into the life and experience of Israel through contact with the Canaanites. In this case the underlying argument would be that sacrifice and cult, however right and proper they may be now if offered with sincerity, are not essential to the life of Israel. If she could live in the wilderness without such things she can do so again now. What is required, both in the wilderness and now, is right behaviour.

The same point about the wilderness period is made by Jeremiah (7:21). What God sought from his people at that time was obedience not sacrifice. So he calls upon his contemporaries ironically to multiply their sacrifices. Yet no matter how much they sacrifice it will be of no avail unless they are obedient. What we cannot be sure about here is whether

Jeremiah is really saying that God does not want sacrifice but obedience, or that God requires obedience as the background to sacrifice. A similar question arises with the statement of Samuel in 1 Samuel 15:22 that 'to obey is better than sacrifice'. At any rate we may be sure that Jeremiah regards sacrifices as discredited and made invalid by injustice, as he says in 6:19-20.

The strength and vigour of the language about sacrifice and worship in Isaiah 1:10-17 is remarkable enough. What the people are now offering to God is an 'abomination' to him and that is a word usually reserved for things or people of great impurity which God cannot tolerate. So their worship has become an intolerable burden to God. It wearies him and he hates it and ignores it. Were it not for verse 15 we may think that here Isaiah is condemning worship outright, but in that verse he has similar things to say about prayer and the spreading forth of the hands, and we can hardly imagine that Isaiah was totally opposed to prayer. More likely it is the prayer and sacrifice and worship of the present disobedient and insincere people which is rejected both by the prophet and by God.

Out of such evidence three views have emerged. First that sacrifice is rejected outright as unnecessary and even wrong. It was not required in the wilderness period when Israel managed without it and it is not required now. What is required is justice and obedience to God without sacrifice. Against this view is the fact that we do find in certain places in the prophetic writings a more positive attitude to the cult which suggests that they did not wish to see the end of it altogether. Second, it may be thought that the prophets appealed for righteousness to undergird sacrifice and claimed that sacrifice without righteousness was hypocritical and indeed sinful. What they looked for then was worship and obedience, not a choice between the two but a proper combination of both inward disposition and outward act. There is much to be said for this point of view. Third, it may be that the prophets regarded worship and sacrifice as perfectly proper, provided that there was this inward disposition of obedience, but that they reacted strongly against any suggestion that worship could be a substitute for God himself.

Acts of worship, however often they may be repeated and

however closely they may follow the regulations laid down in the law, do not of themselves ensure forgiveness or a renewal of relationship with God. In the end only God himself can forgive, for man's relationship with him is personal. He may offer the cult to man as the vehicle for his forgiveness but he is not limited to it or bound by it. The fact that there was no cult in the wilderness period shows that; and so, if necessary, the people of God could get along again without it. Nevertheless, since God has now made this provision of cult and sacrifice, man should use it, recognizing it as a gift from God and bringing to it the humility, righteousness and sincerity that God requires. Only so can the cult be effective in dealing with sin and in ensuring man's proper relationship with God.

12. Prophets among the Temple Staff

The conclusion that the prophets were not opposed to the cult in itself, but only to the cult as understood and practised by their contemporaries would be strengthened considerably if it could be shown that there were prophets who held an official position within the cult as members of the cultic personnel.[82] We hear a good deal in the prophetic books about false prophets who are frequently associated with the royal court, but there are close connections between the court and the cult. At Jerusalem in Judah and at Bethel in Israel the king and his court were much involved in the worship because these were royal sanctuaries. It would not be surprising therefore if the so-called court prophets were also cult prophets and if they functioned not only as givers of advice to the king, but also as cult officials of some sort. Further it would be quite wrong to assume that all these prophets were false.[83] That many were so regarded by the classical prophets cannot be doubted, but there were people like Huldah in the days of Jeremiah (2 Kings 22:14ff.) who apparently held official positions and yet proclaimed the genuine word of God as true prophets.

If we go back again to those fore-runners of the classical prophets it is possible to see that many of them had close connections with the cult. Without repeating all that has been said about Saul's meeting with the band of prophets in 1 Samuel 10:10ff. we may recall that the prophets from whom he 'caught' the spirit of prophecy were coming down from a 'high place' and this is a technical term for a sanctuary. Of course it could be argued that they had only been there, like everyone else, as participants in the worship with no official position in the cult. On the other hand it could equally well be said that they were members of the cultic staff and because of their peculiar inspiration played a more significant part in the worship than the ordinary men who shared in it.

In the days of King David Nathan appears as a court prophet giving advice to the king, yet his concern with the cult is clear enough. His advice to David concerns the building of the temple, first that it should be built and then, later, when he has received another word from Yahweh, that this task should be left to David's successor (2 Sam. 7). Especially in the days of David the court and the cult were inseparable and therefore his prophet would naturally function in both places. Consequently at the enthronement of Solomon we find Zadok the priest and Nathan the prophet side by side sharing in what was undoubtedly a religious ceremony (1 Kings 1:38ff.).

There is no suggestion that Elijah belonged to any group of prophets either at court or within the cult yet at the same time he played a considerable part in the sacrifice on Mount Carmel (1 Kings 18) giving orders about the arrangement of the altar and the sacrificial flesh and eventually calling down fire from Yahweh to consume the sacrifice. The prophets of Baal and Asherah who were in the court of Jezebel were also responsible for the altar and were the main protagonists on the Canaanite side in the struggle between Yahwism and Baalism which took place there. Elijah and the Baal prophets thus played out their contest within the sphere of the cult. Later on Elijah and Elisha met bands of prophets at Bethel and at Jericho. Did it just happen that they lived there? Or was it that these were cultic centres at which the prophets functioned within the cult (2 Kings 2)? Again when the Shunemite woman sent her husband to fetch Elisha to raise her dead son (2 Kings 4:22ff.) the man made the curious reply that it was neither new moon nor feast day. The implication is that he did not know where to find the prophet, except that on these days he could surely be found at the sanctuary. Once more we cannot be sure whether his presence there was simply as a worshipper or whether he was known to be there because he had some part to play in the cult on these special days. The latter is certainly possible and even probable.

When we turn to the classical prophets the evidence for any official connection with the cult is very slight indeed. It is true that the call of Isaiah is couched in strongly cultic terms (Is. 6), but this does not allow us to see him as a cultic prophet. The language may derive simply from his regular participation in the worship in the temple as a prominent layman in Jerusalem and from his intimate knowledge of the temple worship. It is true that he seems to have access to the king easily as though he had some standing in the court and that he married a woman who is described simply as a prophetess in her own right (8:3) but this is quite insufficient evidence to draw any conclusions about his relations with the cult and his teaching gives us no further clue.

Amos deliberately dissociates himself from the bands of prophets who were found at Bethel (7:14). Presumably he preaches there because this is the place where he can reach the maximum number of people with his message. However, Amaziah the priest seems uncertain about his relationship to the groups of prophets who were in Bethel and so there can have been little to distinguish them. In any case the incident shows that there were prophetic bands in Bethel and Bethel is not the royal centre of the Northern Kingdom but the cultic centre, the royal court and palace being at Samaria. There is again some evidence for prophets associated with the cult even if Amos himself was not one of them.

Hosea and Micah seem to have no connection at all with the cult unless Hosea's wife was a cult prostitute. Even then that says nothing about Hosea's own standing in the cult. Jeremiah is said to have lived among the priests at Anathoth (1:1) and this may indicate that he belonged to a priestly family. In any case these priests would not have been functioning in Anathoth after 621 BC for in that year all worship was centralized in Jerusalem. Any connection with the priesthood is at this personal level and there is no suggestion anywhere that Jeremiah held any official position within the cult. Indeed the fact that Josiah consulted Huldah the prophetess and not Jeremiah about the Law Book points clearly in the opposite direction (2 Kings 22:14ff.). On occasion Jeremiah preached in the temple court (ch. 7) but it was open to anyone to do so and this was the place where people gathered in large numbers for the festivals. Others who have connections with the priesthood are Ezekiel and Zechariah. The former is a priest become prophet (1:3) when he is cut off from the temple where he might have expected to exercise his priestly ministry. This is very different from being a prophet with a special role to play within the cult.

The teaching of Nahum and Obadiah is peculiarly nationalistic. Nahum announces with glee the downfall of Nineveh in a manner which reminds us of the nationalistic prophets such as Hananiah (Jer. 27 and 28). The first ten verses of the book are in the form of an acrostic hymn celebrating the theophany, the appearing of Yahweh. Both the form and content remind us of the psalms and on the basis of this it is sometimes argued that Nahum was a cult prophet. Similarly Obadiah may possibly have been one of those nationalistic prophets left behind in Judah after the deportation of the Jewish leaders to Babylon who continued to threaten Israel's enemies, in this case Edom.

More than this we cannot say about the classical prophets. The books in their present form do contain cultic material comparable with the psalms. Not only is this true of Nahum, but also of Habakkuk and Isaiah and Jonah. In view of what we have said about the collection and preservation of the prophetic oracles this should not surprise us. It is virtually certain that these oracles were later recited in worship, perhaps even as early as the exilic period when the spoken elements of the cult were developed at the expense of the acted parts which could no longer be performed because of the separation from the temple. At this stage psalm-like, liturgical additions were made to the collections and consequently these offer no evidence at all for the connection of the prophet himself with the cult.

Evidence for prophets at work in the cult really comes from a different source altogether, namely from the psalms. Within some of these there is material which is in the oracular, prophetic style and form. Several of these psalms belong to the ceremony of the royal enthronement and take us back to the part which Nathan played first in David's affairs and then in Solomon's accession and coronation (1 Kings 1). Though the anointing was done by Zadok the priest, Nathan is at his side and his presence is obviously important. Early in the reign of Solomon Nathan seems to have disappeared.

Whether he had died we cannot say. But his son is listed among Solomon's priests and as a 'king's friend' (1 Kings 4:5).

Psalm 89 celebrates the Davidic kingship and was probably used at the accession of the new king and at his enthronement. The divine promises to the new king are made by a 'faithful one' (v. 19) on the basis of a vision he has received. Just as the new king is the successor of David so this 'faithful one' is the successor of Nathan and performs exactly the same functions as that prophet, doing so within the cult. Psalm 2 falls into the same category of enthronement psalms. This includes the divine decree by which the king rules and the king is adopted as the 'son of God'. This takes us right back again to Nathan's oracle to David in 2 Samuel 7:14 in which God promises to be his father and to make David his son. Psalm 110 is a difficult psalm with its reference to Melchizedek, but it will be sufficient here to point out that the psalm begins with a similar promise to the king and this is introduced by the prophetic formula 'the LORD says'. In all three of these psalms we may see a prophet at work in the manner of Nathan, taking his part in the cultic ceremony of enthronement.

Psalm 132 is of a rather different type. It celebrates the bringing of the ark to Jerusalem in 2 Samuel 6. It should be seen, however, not simply as a psalm for that specific occasion but as a psalm to be used in later regular celebrations of what David had done. In v. 11 there is a promise to David, that is, to the king of the Davidic dynasty whoever he may be at the time and this promise reiterates that made to David by Nathan. We may therefore assume that its re-affirmation is made by a prophet, a successor of Nathan, who thus has a clear function within the cult.

The work of such cultic prophets was not restricted to enthronement ceremonies. Their oracles can be discerned in other of the psalms. Psalm 52:1-7 might have come straight out of one of the prophetic books for it is a condemnation of those who reject the steadfast love of God and those who love evil more than good. The same harsh word of judgement is found in v. 5 as appears in the prophetic books. Whoever the speaker is he contrasts himself with the people whom he addresses and then claims to be among the 'godly' (v. 9). The

Hebrew word used here is precisely that which is used of the prophet in Psalm 89:19 where RSV has translated 'faithful one'.

Psalm 95 celebrates the kingship of Yahweh. It consists of a double call to worship which has made some scholars suspicious about the unity of the psalm. More recently the psalm has been seen to be part of a liturgy in which vv. 1-5 invite the people into the temple courts and vv. 5-7 invite them into the sanctuary proper.[84] Vv. 8-11 are not then to be detached (as they often are in practice) but are an integral part of the liturgy in which a prophet recalls people to loyalty to Yahweh who is proclaimed king, the whole tone of this section being strikingly prophetic.[85]

Finally the late book of Chronicles provides some interesting references. 1 Chronicles 25:1-6 says that the sons of Asaph, who were singers in the temple, *prophesied* under the direction of the king (v. 2). Similarly in 2 Chronicles 20 the spirit of the LORD came upon a Levite, a son of Asaph, so that he prophesied to king Jehoshaphat advising him to go out to battle for God who would give him victory, just as the prophets of his northern contemporary Ahab had advised him to fight the Syrians but with a happier outcome! In 2 Chronicles 29:30 and 35:15 Asaph and Jeduthun are described as seers. By the 4th century BC, then, and probably much earlier, certain cultic officials could be described as prophets or seers.

The evidence brought forward in this chapter is cumulative. Many of the references, taken separately, can be explained otherwise than by postulating an official position of prophet within the cult. But when it is all put together it does seem likely that, in addition to those men who stood out as individuals to proclaim the word of God to as many as would hear it, there were others, some in the king's court and some working within the cult, who were also regarded as prophets. No doubt some of these were mere 'professionals' who did no more than speak the word they believed the king and people wished to hear. We should not assume, however, that they all fell into this category. There were probably men and women who, within the structures of Israel's worship, sought to hear the word of God and to proclaim it faithfully to the best of their ability.

13. Prophets and Wise Men

There is always the danger of isolating the prophets from their fellows and seeing them in opposition to such groups as the priests. Often they were, but just as there were good and bad prophets in Israel so there were also good and bad priests. The good priests do not stand in opposition to the prophets and, as we have seen, the prophets did not have a wholly negative attitude towards the work which the priests were doing. But there is also a third recognizable group of people in Israel, known as the Wise Men!

The three groups are mentioned together in Jeremiah 18:18, along with their respective functions. The priests' task is to teach the law of God, the prophets' task is to declare the word of God and the task of the Wise Men is to give counsel or advice. If we ask what is the difference between the word of God declared by the prophet and the counsel which is given by the Wise Men the answer is that the word of God comes directly to the prophet through his inspiration, whereas the advice of the Wise Men is the result of their observation and understanding of life. Hence, they are sometimes misleadingly called the humanists of the Old Testament. Yet prophets and wise men are no more necessarily opposed to each other than are prophets and priests and there seem to be points of contact between the two.

In order to see this it is necessary to digress a little so as to understand the nature and characteristics of the Wisdom Literature of the Old Testament, bearing in mind that this term may be applied to everything from a statement like

> Like a gold ring in a swine's snout
> is a beautiful woman without discretion (Prov. 11:22)

to the book of Job with all its wrestling with the profound questions of life and experience.[86]

Like all peoples Israel observed life and experience as it

was and certain people tried to encapsulate it in short, pithy sayings. Out of these observations the Wise Men formulated general principles of life and so helped to make life manageable, just as do some of our English proverbs such as 'a rolling stone gathers no moss' with the implied advice not to become a rolling stone. So Israel's wise men observed that

He who tills his land will have plenty of bread

and is able to follow this with the further statement that

He who follows worthless pursuits has no sense
(Prov. 12:11).

It can hardly be thought that the Israelites regarded these statement as invariably true in all circumstances.

No ill befalls the righteous
But the wicked are filled with trouble (Prov. 12:21)

may have been largely true but surely there was never a time when this was universally true and the Wise Men can scarcely have been blind to the exceptions which were there to be seen. However, it is sufficiently true to be a serviceable principle on which to build one's life. They therefore become equivalent to a piece of advice and are a way of saying 'be industrious!' or 'be righteous!' They are best understood as pieces of advice rather than as statements of fact.

Such sayings were then used in the education of young men, sometimes within the family setting, but often in 'schools' for training young men in leadership either at home or abroad. they may even have served as copy-book material for those learning to write, at the same time helping them to understand the principles of successful living. We have little direct evidence of such 'schools' in Israel, though passages like Isaiah 29:14 and Jeremiah 18:18 may point in that direction. In Proverbs 1:9 a father addresses his sons but in all probability this is not a family relationship but a teacher–pupil one. The 'sons' of the Wise Man are the pupils just as the 'sons of the prophets' are the prophetic groups. By 'schools' we do not mean to imply that there was a general system of education in early Israel. More likely the 'pupils' were young men of noble birth who were destined to share in the government of their people or to represent Israel overseas in diplomacy or commerce. They were thus closely linked with the royal court (Prov. 25:1). Similar schools were in existence in other countries such as Egypt and Mesopotamia and it was therefore essential for those who went abroad, for example in the reign of Solomon when he had many diplomatic and commercial interests in different parts of the Near East, to know these principles of living which were universally valid. At the same time these people brought back with them sayings which had been coined in other countries. In this way wisdom writings have a certain international flavour about them.

It is noticeable when reading a book like Proverbs how rarely the word 'God' or 'Lord' appears and it could be thought that for the Wise Men Yahweh had no place in the affairs of the world. Yet here and there God does appear, and sometimes in proverbs which are very similar to Egyptian ones as, for example, in Proverbs 11:1

> A false balance is an abomination to the Lord
> but a just weight is his delight.

These occasional references to God indicate that for the Wise Men as for other Israelites the whole scheme of nature was not independent of God. Rather, every event and circumstance was ultimately controlled by him whether or not this was made explicit. It would be surprising if it were otherwise for these Wise Men were Israelites who must have been familiar with the great national traditions of Israel, recited both in their homes and in their worship, in which Yahweh's control of all things was firmly expressed. Consequently there is a saying which occurs several times in slightly differing forms. In Proverbs 1:7 it takes the form

> The fear of the Lord is the beginning of knowledge.

The word translated 'beginning' also carries with it the idea of 'foundation' and so the fundamental basis of all knowledge or wisdom is to be found in the 'fear of the Lord' which means a truly religious attitude of reverence and obedience towards God. Thus the whole wisdom tradition had its roots in religion, just like everything else in Israel.

90

Further, any wisdom which a man gains through his observation of the world is ultimately a gift from God who alone is wise and who alone gives wisdom. Men may therefore be urged to get wisdom (Prov. 4:5ff.), but it can only be obtained by maintaining this proper relationship with God. Wisdom itself is sometimes personified. She is with God and has been with him from the very beginning (Prov. 8:22-31) and so anyone who wishes to acquire it must do so from God. This means that a truly 'religious' life is essential for the proper understanding of the 'secular' life in which man lives day by day.

There emerged from these schools certain stories, sometimes called *novelles*. They may or may not be based on historical events, but they tell the story with very little reference to God. Three such *novelles* are to be found in the Joseph stories (Gen. 37–47), the story of the struggles to succeed David (2 Sam. 9–1 Kings 2) and the Daniel stories (Dan. 1–6). In the Joseph and Daniel stories there is an amazing tolerance of foreign ideas and practices illustrating the international nature of the literature. In both stories a man becomes highly successful in life and rises to high position in a foreign court. Underlying this success is wisdom which is openly acknowledged to be a gift from God. In the narrative about the succession of David the impression is left that events are running their course quite independently of God except that in one or two places (2 Sam. 11:27, 12:24) God, as it were, comes to the surface and so reveals that he has been at work below the surface all the time directing affairs in the direction he wishes them to take.

At a later stage it seems as though some of these pieces of advice which were meant to give guidance for living had come to be regarded as absolute statements of fact. So, 'No ill befalls the righteous' became a sort of dogma on the basis of which it could be said that if a man suffered misfortune then it must be due to his sin. This is the problem which was tackled in the books of Job and Ecclesiastes. Job especially rejects this way of looking at things and refuses to accept that a man's morality and attitude to God can necessarily be deduced from the circumstances of his life.

Now this summary of the wisdom literature at once reveals

certain fundamental differences between the wisdom and the prophetic ways of looking at life. The former has a much more 'secular' feel about it; it carries no references to the cult either supporting or opposing it; there is no mention of those ancient traditions of Israel and Judah which the prophets used so extensively, the exodus, the promised land, David or Jerusalem; the idea of divine judgement of the nation does not occur; the whole literature is intensely personal and individual and makes no reference to the great historic moments in the life of the people of God. As a result wisdom and prophecy are often set at opposite poles. But it is a mistake to see these as separate groups in Israel and Judah who have nothing in common and who never meet. Isaiah 29:14 may suggest such a sharp division and even confrontation between them, but this was a sharp difference of opinion about the policy to be adopted by Judah and the king at that particular moment, rather than a fundamental antagonism between two parties. There were occasions when the prophets differed from all those around them, priests, Wise Men and rulers but this does not allow us to set them in constant opposition. (Cf. Jer. 8:8ff. where they are coupled with priests and false prophets.)

Indeed, it is possible to see certain points of contact between the Wise Men and the prophets or, to put it more accurately, to see the influence of wisdom teaching in the prophetic books. This is not to be wondered at if some of the wisdom teaching was formulated not only in the 'schools' but also in the homes and in local societies where the prophets were brought up. In any case the wisdom 'schools' and some of the prophets must have lived in close proximity, for instance in the court at Jerusalem.

Proverbs 25:1 makes it clear that sayings were collected by the men of Hezekiah, that is, in his court. Yet we know that Isaiah had easy access to Hezekiah and must therefore have been familiar enough with that same court, whether or not he lived at court. So there are passages in Isaiah which do remind us of the wisdom writings. Isaiah 10:15,

> Shall the axe vaunt itself over him that hews with it,
> or the saw magnify itself against him who wields it?

is a popular riddle such as are mentioned in Proverbs 1:6 as part of the stock in trade of the Wise Men.

But it is especially in that part of the book which deals with the reign of Hezekiah that echoes of the wisdom literature are to be found. The 'scoffers' mentioned in 28:14, and 29:20 in conjunction with the 'ruthless' are familiar to us from books like Proverbs. The importance of 'understanding' and 'instruction' (29:24) corresponds to the place these have in the wisdom writings. In 28:20 there is another popular saying or proverb, while 28:24-29 offers a piece of teaching in the question and answer method of the wisdom schools and stresses that counsel and wisdom come from God. It would, of course, go far beyond the evidence to suggest that Isaiah was a Wise Man turned prophet, but at this point in his ministry at any rate there is a stock of ideas and vocabulary which he holds in common with the Wise Men and which he no doubt acquired as a result of his common environment with them in Jerusalem.

This explanation will not do for Amos who also shows signs of being aware of wisdom teaching. He was not from Jerusalem but from Tekoa, not from the city but from a town on the fringes of the wilderness to the west of the Dead Sea. But in 2 Samuel 14:2 we are told that David's general, Joab, sent to Tekoa to fetch a wise woman to persuade David to recall Absalom. From this it is sometimes thought that Tekoa was a place famous for its wisdom 'school'. If this were so it would explain why Amos seems to use the methods of speaking which were found in the wisdom tradition. The numerical sayings which run through chapter 1 into chapter 2 each beginning, 'For three transgressions of ..., and for four ...' were used in the schools (cf. Prov. 30:15ff.), as was the argument by means of rhetorical questions as found in Amos 3:3-8. Again we have insufficient evidence to say that Amos was associated in some direct way with wisdom circles in Tekoa; we can only suggest that he lived in an environment where this way of speaking was common and became familiar with it there.

All this may be enough to show that in the Old Testament there are two different approaches to life. One begins from the national theology and from a personal experience of God which constitutes a call and goes on to apply these to the particular situations in the life of the nation in which the person lives; this is the prophetic. The other begins from everyday life and experience and finds in it certain firm principles upon which the individual may base his conduct with a view to making a success of life, recognizing these to be part of the activity of God in his world; this is wisdom. Both these are found in the Old Testament. They influence each other and overlap here and there because the men who hold them do not live in separate compartments, but side by side in a common environment. In many cases they come to similar conclusions though they may be differently expressed. Wisdom's 'No ill shall befall the righteous' (Prov. 12:21) may find its prophetic counterpart in Amos' 'Seek good and not evil, that you may live' (5:14) or in Hosea's 'Woe to them for they have strayed from me' (7:13). Yet in certain times of crisis there could be a deep rift between the two and strong opposition between them. The advice of the Wise, just like the teaching of the priests or the word of the court prophet (Jer. 18:18) could, in the eyes of the classical prophet with his own deep individual experience of God, be regarded as contradicting the will of God and diverting the people from his way. They were thus ripe for destruction.

14. Towards Apocalyptic

Justification for the inclusion of a chapter on apocalyptic in a book about prophecy lies in the fact that the book of Daniel, which is usually regarded as apocalyptic, is now placed among the prophetic books in the English Bible, though not in the Hebrew Bible where it is included amongst the Writings. But also there are some links between prophecy and apocalyptic which it is useful to trace. They differ from the links between prophecy and wisdom which can be put down to a similar environment, because the apocalyptists were not contemporary with the prophets, they lived and worked much later. This is why this chapter is headed '*Towards* Apocalyptic'. In the main the apocalyptic writings fall between Daniel which is a book from the 2nd century BC and Revelation in the 2nd century AD; that is, they fall mainly in the inter-testamental and the New Testament period. There are one or two other Old Testament passages which bear similar marks such as Isaiah 24–27 and Zechariah 9–14 though it is going too far to describe these as apocalypses.

When seeking a definition of apocalyptic[87] the tendency is to examine the book of Daniel to discover its salient features. Having defined apocalyptic in that way the claim is not surprisingly made that Daniel is apocalyptic! It is easy to fall into the trap of this circular argument. A close examination of Daniel, however, reveals very strong associations with the wisdom literature which we have already mentioned. This is especially apparent in chapters 1–6 which bear strong resemblance to the Joseph stories of Genesis 37–47. But even in the later chapters 7–12 the concern with the whole world as experienced and the absence of concern with the peculiarly Israelite traditions points in the same direction. So it is not to be wondered at that some scholars have seen Daniel as a later development of the wisdom schools.[88] Others, however, have regarded this as too restricted a view.[89]

It is not easy to characterize apocalyptic, therefore, but

certain points may be made remembering that Daniel stands at the beginning of a process and bearing in mind that warning given about the circular argument. The first thing that strikes the reader is the extremely rich and often puzzling symbolism which presupposes a literary tradition and not an oral one. It is hard to think of, say, Daniel 7 being preached; it is too carefully thought out and its imagery is too complicated to have been invented and used orally. In so far as it is written rather than spoken it may be thought to have its links with Wisdom rather than with prophecy. Yet, at the same time, the predecessor of such symbolism is to be found in the opening chapters of Ezekiel so that links with prophecy are by no means ruled out.

Another feature of apocalyptic is that it is pseudonymous, being written under an assumed name. We need not go into the reason for this here. It is sufficient to note the fact, for in this respect it differs from both prophecy and wisdom. Many of the prophetic books come from people whose names we know while some are anonymous. The wisdom literature is largely anonymous too, but neither are pseudonymous. Some wisdom is attributed to Solomon, however, though certainly he was not personally responsible for it. But by being ascribed to him it gained a certain authority. In the same way some apocalyptic works are attributed to figures of the more distant past, partly to provide authority for them, but also so that they may be presented as future predictions now coming to their fulfilment. The element of prediction is therefore prominent in apocalyptic and this belongs to prophecy and not to wisdom where it has no part at all. The future predicted, however, seems to be one which intrudes upon the earth from outside rather than, as in the prophets, the outcome of historical process.

Its view of history is quite deterministic, not only with regard to Israel, but with regard to the whole world. Great world empires rise and fall by the will of God, not simply as the context in which to set the life and conduct of Israel or Judah but because the concern is quite universal. All this history, presented of course as future, culminates in the intervention of God in the final day, which is imminent. This new age is the one in which Israel will be supreme.

It may be seen from this how complicated is the relationship between wisdom, prophecy and apocalyptic. N. W. Porteous[90] says, 'It may have incorporated wisdom material, that is to say, stories which might have been used to illustrate general truths about life, but, as we have them, the accent of impending crisis rests upon them. Something of the old prophetic inspiration is present again confronting the challenge of a new day.' Certainly apocalyptic owes something to both prophecy and wisdom. It is the debt to prophecy which we shall look at mainly here.[91]

Prophecy came to an end. We cannot put a firm date upon this end but we may say with some certainty that it came soon after 400 BC.[92] The end of the book of Malachi suggests this with its hopeful anticipation of a new Elijah, that is, a resumption of prophetic inspiration. We have already seen how the prophetic canon was closed by 190 BC and how Jewish tradition thought of the prophetic era ending about the time of Ezra (c. 400 BC). 1 Maccabees 4:46 also looks forward to the emergence of a prophet in the 2nd century BC. No such prophet arose, but the book of Daniel may confidently be placed in this period and may be regarded, in a sense, as a substitute for prophecy in those critical days of Antiochus Epiphanes when the Jews and their religion were threatened with extinction. Early apocalyptic may thus have served the purpose which had been served by prophecy in earlier days still.

Prophecy and apocalyptic, then, have a number of features in common. Both show a deep concern for the will of God and for loyalty to it in the contemporary situation. The prophets warn those who have become disloyal to Yahweh of the result of their disloyalty and from time to time appeal to them for repentance and for renewed obedience to his will. Though the situation is different with the apocalyptists the same concern is there. At the time of the book of Daniel the Jewish religion was proscribed and the Jews were forbidden to carry out their time-honoured practices. This was a new situation. In earlier times there had been great pressures from other nations to introduce the worship of foreign gods and there had been a good deal of syncretism, for example, under the reign of Manasseh when the Assyrians were in control of Judah, but never had the worship of Yahweh been totally forbidden as it was by Antiochus Epiphanes, the ruler of the Seleucid kingdom to the north of Judah in the 2nd century BC. He destroyed the city of Jerusalem and defiled the temple. He compelled people to sacrifice to himself as god and ordered the destruction of all copies of the Jewish Law. This was something new and it raised the question of loyalty in a new and sharper form. There were many who found it impossible to remain loyal, for to do so meant death. The books of Maccabees, for instance 2 Maccabees 6:10ff., indicate the fate of those who sought to maintain their traditional faith in face of the new regulations. One of the primary purposes of the book of Daniel was therefore to encourage those people who made such a stand and to strengthen the resolve of those who defied Antiochus, by continuing to worship Yahweh. In its own way, therefore, the apocalyptic book of Daniel continues the tradition of calling for loyalty to Yahweh which characterized the prophets.

In both cases this call for loyalty was rooted in the past experience of the people. The prophets pointed to what Yahweh had done for his people in the exodus or the choice of David and Jerusalem. The apocalyptists based their call on different traditions of the past which are not found outside their works. They presented history in a schematized way. There had been four great world empires, represented in Daniel 7 by the four beasts coming out of the sea. Each one had been fierce and terrible, but they had all been under the control of God in the last resort and he had brought each to an end. So the present tyranny would be brought to an end by God just as the previous ones had been, for he is in control of all history. This past history which they recalled in strange symbols bore little relation to what we should call history and was quite different from the history to which the prophets referred. It may have been based on foreign models, perhaps from Persia, but its concern was to assert the sovereignty of God and to overlook this is to miss the whole point of the book of Daniel. At the same time, even this idea of God's control of the nations and empires of the world is not unknown among the prophets for Amos (chs. 1 and 2) had asserted that all the nations surrounding Israel were accountable to God for their actions; Isaiah (10:5) had asserted that the Assyrians were being used as the instrument of God for the punishment of Judah and they would be discarded when God's purpose of judgement had been fulfilled; the prophet of the exile (Is. 44:28, 45:1f.) had claimed that God was raising up Cyrus to bring down the Babylonian empire so that the Jews may be allowed to return to their homeland. Thus the idea that nations are under the control of God is nothing new, though the manner in which the past history is presented is. But if God is so in control of world events then the Jews need have no fear and should remain loyal to this universally powerful God.

So both prophecy and apocalyptic are both deeply concerned with contemporary affairs and seek in their different ways to present a picture of an all-powerful God who can and will handle the present situation for the good of his people. They both, consequently, make predictions about the imminent future and they both insist that this future is possible only because God will bring it about. So far as the prophets are concerned God will judge Israel and Judah, bringing to an end his present relationship with them. But after that, by another act of free choice and grace, he will call them once again to be his people, bringing them back from exile by a second exodus (Is. 40–55), making with them a new covenant (Jer. 31:31f., Ezek. 36:24ff.) or raising up a new David for them (Is. 9:2-7, 11:1-9). For the writer of Daniel, on the other hand, God will judge the nations which oppress Israel and will give authority to the Son of Man. There has been a great deal of discussion about the identity of this Son of Man[93] and we cannot even summarize it here. The view we take is that it refers to the new corporate Israel who, under God, will have dominion over the earth and this will be due entirely to the activity of God. Though the future hope may be expressed in different terms by the prophets and the apocalyptists there is a fundamental similarity in the way they look forward to what God will do.

We have already pointed out how the Day of Yahweh underwent a fresh and negative interpretation by the prophets and yet there still remained a 'day to come' which would be a great day for Israel. Sometimes when the prophets tried to draw a picture of this day they did so in symbolic terms. In Isaiah 11:1-9 the healing of the broken relationship by God would extend also to the animal kingdom. For Joel the beasts of the field and the pastures upon which they feed will rejoice (2:21f.) while the mountains will drip milk and flow with wine (3:18). Ezekiel had already spoken in highly symbolic language of Yahweh leaving Jerusalem and then returning to it (43:3) and the theme of the destruction of foreign nations and the elevation of Judah over them had its place in the prophetic hopes (Is. 2:1-4). It is this latter theme which is taken up and elaborated by the apocalyptists in a picture of the future painted in vivid colours.

There was also a further development. The new ruler envisaged by the prophets may be a new earthly king comparable with David of the past. He is an earthly figure raised up by God. In Daniel, too, the Son of Man is an earthly figure who comes *to* the Ancient of Days (Dan. 7:13), though here, as noted above, this is probably a symbol for corporate Israel rather than an individual ruler. But in later apocalyptic the Son of Man becomes not a human figure coming *to* the Ancient of Days, but a semi-divine figure coming from him and riding on the clouds (1 Enoch and Mark 13:24ff.).

It would be a mistake, then, to draw too rigid a distinction between prophecy and apocalyptic. Certainly other streams beside prophecy have flowed in it from the wisdom tradition and from Persian mythology. But allowing for the new situation and for the fact that the prophetic canon was closed, many of the old prophetic concerns do find expression in new form in the book of Daniel and in this whole type of literature called apocalyptic. In view of this the inclusion of small passages resembling apocalyptic into the prophetic books (e.g. Is. 24–27) is understandable.

IV
Prophetic Teaching

15.   God's Holiness and Man's

We turn now from examining the relationship between prophecy and other strands of Old Testament writing to looking more closely at some of the main themes of prophetic teaching. Of these the holiness of God stands out clearly. What is meant by this can perhaps be seen by comparing two texts from Amos. In chapter 4:2 God is said to swear by his holiness, while in 6:8 he swears by himself. Oaths such as these are dependent for their efficacy upon the person or thing which is invoked. It is important therefore that this person or thing should be more powerful than the person swearing the oath; otherwise there would be no point in invoking him. So a man may swear by the life of the king (2 Sam. 11:11) or even by the life of Yahweh himself if the swearer happens to be a king (2 Sam. 12:5). But by whom may Yahweh swear to validate his oath? There is no-one greater and he cannot swear by anyone less. Therefore, in Amos 6:8, he swears by his 'self', his own very being. Consequently when he swears by his holiness (Amos 4:2) this cannot refer to a part of God or even a quality of God; it also must refer to God himself in his divinity. So holiness is not just one quality of God among others; it stands for his divine being in its fulness, for God distinct from man and elevated far above him.

The etymology of the word, for what it is worth, points in the same direction.[94] Some see its underlying meaning as 'to cut' or 'to separate'; others see it as meaning 'to be brilliant' and therefore needing to be screened from eyes which cannot tolerate it. It is therefore said to refer to the idea of separation in one way or the other and, when used of God, to refer to his separateness in his exaltation above men.

The title 'Holy One of Israel' is characteristic of all parts of the book of Isaiah. It occurs some thirty times within the book and only some eleven times outside it. So it is primarily, though not exclusively, to Isaiah that we look for our under-standing of the holiness of God, at least so far as the prophets are concerned. Perhaps his frequent use of this term is due to his vision in chapter 6 which we have previously discussed. The unapproachable divinity of God is expressed in the super-lative 'Holy, holy, holy', sung by the seraphim and Isaiah at once becomes aware of the enormous gap which separates him from God. It is not only his 'unclean lips' which separate him from God. They are simply the part of him which focus the distinction. He, as man, has seen God in his full power and authority as the divine king and so feels 'undone' not because he fears God will punish his sin, but because he has entered into the destructive field of God's holiness from which there is no escape. Just as Uzzah (2 Sam. 6:6ff.) was struck dead by the holiness of Yahweh transmitted through the ark, so now Isaiah can expect only the same fate. Indeed it is possible that the ark was, in some way, involved in this vision. However that may be, the next stage in the vision clearly indicates the possibility of a relationship between this holy God and man, for Isaiah is cleansed and made fit to be used by God. This is then reflected in his affirmation that Yahweh is the 'Holy One *of Israel*'. In other words there is a special relationship be-tween the Holy One and his people Israel which makes Israel a 'holy people' too.

Even though the word is not used at all in the description of Ezekiel's vision in chapter 1 the idea certainly permeates it. What does this strange vision signify if not the utter divinity of God and his complete otherness from men. So aware is Ezekiel of this that he cannot here speak directly of God, or even of his 'glory' which is the self-revelation of his divine nature, or even of the 'likeness of the glory of God', but only of the 'appearance of the likeness of the glory of God'. So far removed from man is God and, as in the case of Isaiah, the result is totally overwhelming. Ezekiel fell upon his face and was powerless to rise unless God by his call spoke across the gap and called him to rise. Thereafter Ezekiel speaks not so much about the glory of God but rather about his 'holy name' (20:39 etc.) where the name represents the very person of God as well as his reputation. God's name has been profaned, made unholy and brought into disrepute by Judah's sin

104

(36:20) and when he restores the people it will be for the sake of his holy name (36:21). By what he does with Israel God will make his name known not only in Israel but among all nations (39:7) and here Ezekiel can use Isaiah's phrase, the 'holy one'.

The prophet of the exile picks up the phrase again, as we might expect, and uses it frequently. Yahweh is the 'holy one' (Is. 40:25) who by his own divine power has created all things. In comparison with him the great nations of the world are like the drops that hang from a bucket after it has been filled with water. Men are like grasshoppers. He is everlasting, the creator of the ends of the earth. The gap which separates him from man in wisdom, power and authority could hardly be wider. But he is the 'holy one', too, because it is he who has redeemed Israel (43:3, 14f., 45:11, 54:5), who brings them back home (41:17ff.) and so creates Israel all over again (45:11). Again the gap is between redeemer and redeemed, creator and created and thus the sheer dependence of Israel upon God is stressed. In the third part of this book God's ways and thoughts are higher than man's by as much as the heavens are higher than the earth (55:9).

All this rules out human pride which by itself seeks to build a ladder into the divine sphere. It is not only condemned by the prophets, but is doomed to failure in the very nature of the case (Is. 2:12). For the same reason reliance on human helpers such as the Egyptians is foolish and useless; they are men not God (31:3). God is God and man is man and so it must remain.

Now this holiness can in certain circumstances be conferred upon things and upon men through the relationship which God establishes freely with them. Thus they are 'consecrated'; that is, 'made holy'. The ark, contact with which caused the death of Uzzah, and the priests who are 'set aside' are 'drawn into the field' of God's holiness and themselves become holy. They are thus capable of closer contact with the holy God and, at the same time, more dangerous to others who may come into contact with them because they bear this holiness which has its origin in God. There is good reason for believing that during the exile and among the priests the idea of holiness moved towards that of ritual cleanliness, though it still retains its notion of being set apart. In Ezekiel 45:1f. a district of Israel is set apart as holy to Yahweh. The chambers of the priests in the rebuilt temple will be holy (46:19 etc.). In this sense the word is now used in those parts of the prophetic books which come closest to priestly teaching. There is considerable doubt whether chapters 40–48 of Ezekiel were spoken or written by that prophet and yet it is here that the word 'holy' occurs no less than seventeen times.

The same concern with purity is to be found in Haggai. The precise interpretation of 2:10-19 is uncertain,[95] but we are dealing with a priestly oracle of some sort. Either the priests are saying that unholy people will make the temple unholy rather than the holiness of the temple being conveyed to the unholy builders, or that the worship being offered defiles the temple because of its impurity rather than the temple sanctifying the impure offering. In either case what is at stake is the holiness or purity of the temple which Haggai is concerned to maintain.

The holiness of the temple and of the hill upon which it stands, Zion, is a common theme in those prophetic writings which come from the exilic period or later (Is. 57:13, 65:11, 65:25, 66:20, Obad. 16, Zech. 8:3, Joel 2:1, 3:17). These owe their holiness to the fact that God either dwells or manifests himself upon them and so communicates his holiness to them to a degree. There was current in the ancient world the belief that the gods lived on holy mountains, Baal in Zaphon and, later, the Greek gods on Mount Olympus. It was possible for this idea to be taken up in Israel and naturally the mount of God would be identified as Zion (cf. Is. 2:1-4, Ezek. 28:14). But in addition the Deuteronomists had spoken of Zion as the place where God makes his name to dwell and this gave to it its sanctity.

Israel had already been described as a 'holy nation', set apart for God, in Exodus 19:5, yet this expression is not found among the pre-exilic prophets. They seem to prefer other terminology. Israel is called and chosen. God 'knows' them (Amos 3:2) and thus they are separated from other nations. It is found in a later post-exilic prophecy in Isaiah 62:12 which speaks of the new redeemed community in the same terms as are applied to those redeemed from Egypt in

Exodus 19:5. We may expect to find it also in Ezekiel 40–48 and indeed in 44:9 there is the rather negative expression that only the holy people and no foreigners will be allowed to enter the sanctuary. In other words the same point is being made as is perhaps made by Haggai 2:10-19. These few references will indicate that it is not common for the prophets to speak of Israel as the 'holy nation'. This leaves room for some of them to see Israel as responsible for showing God to other nations, not in any outward missionary activity but in allowing God's holiness and his holy name to be seen by other nations (Ezek. 36:22, Is. 40:3f.) in her life and experience.

It may be thought that this prominent idea of a holy God would make impossible any real relationship with people who did not in some way share this holiness. One means by which that relationship may be established and maintained was through the cult which God had provided for that purpose. If our conclusions in chapter 11 are correct then we have to say that the prophets too recognized the value of the cult in this respect. But they did not regard it as the only way in which God and man could be brought together. The calls of Isaiah and Ezekiel make it abundantly clear that God could move towards man without the cult by cleansing the lips of Isaiah and by setting Ezekiel upon his feet. Further, God's holiness, his own nature and being, is expressed in righteousness and devotion (Is. 5:16) and man's response in these same terms may assure him of access to God. So Micah 6:6ff. claims that it is not an abundance of sacrifice which God wants but 'justice, kindness and humility before God'.

Finally there is one passage in Zechariah 14:20, a late passage, which looks towards the future age when everything will have been taken up into the sphere of God's holiness, even the bells on the horses and the pots and pans in the temple! Even here, however, the distinction between God and man is not blurred. It simply means that when all men come to worship God in the temple at the Feast of Tabernacles everything will have been sanctified, lifted into the sphere of divine holiness, so that their worship may be acceptable. Universalism requires universal holiness so that all men may come near to worship God.

16. Righteousness and Sin

The call of Isaiah (ch. 6) establishes a certain link between holiness and righteousness. The overwhelming sense of God's holiness makes the prophet conscious not only of his own and his people's humanity, but also of the fact that their lips are unclean. This does not mean that righteousness is a constituent element of holiness or that holiness is just another attribute alongside righteousness. Holiness is God's divine nature and according to Isaiah (5:16) this finds true expression in righteousness. His holiness and exaltation are vindicated by his righteousness and justice. These qualities are contrasted with man's pride by which he seeks to become God, taking charge of his own affairs, and which is the root of all sin (Is. 5:15).

So now we need to look at four terms which declare something of God's holy nature. The first is this word 'righteousness'.[96] Although it is a very common Old Testament word it occurs less frequently in the prophetic books than we might expect, especially as an attribute of God. The word indicates the kind of behaviour that may be expected not because of a set of rules laid down, but because of a relationship which exists between two persons. So, to speak of the righteousness of God is not to say that there are certain well-defined rules governing his behaviour which he obeys. Rather it indicates what he does and ought to do for those people whom he has chosen as his own simply because he has called them. Jeremiah (12:1) having been called to serve God by declaring his word, feels that he has been let down by God since he suffers in the performance of his task while wicked men, who fail to obey God, prosper. There would be no problem in this for Jeremiah if he did not still believe that God was righteous, that is to say, has certain obligations towards the man he has called. He finds it difficult to reconcile these two things: on the one hand the righteousness of God in which he firmly believes and, on the other, the experiences through which he is passing as a servant of God.

Above all the righteousness of God is seen in his dealings with Israel, his chosen people. This relationship imposes upon God an obligation to help and save his people. Consequently the word which is usually translated 'righteousness' is rendered 'saving acts' in the RSV in Micah 6:5. His 'righteousnesses' are the acts by which he saves Israel from her enemies. In Isaiah 45:13 God's raising up of Cyrus to deliver Israel is an act of righteousness, while in Isaiah 51:5f. it is parallel with 'salvation' and so is translated 'deliverance' in the RSV. Finally the ideal future king empowered by the spirit of God will manifest God's righteousness on earth (Is. 11:1f.). Thus God reveals his god-ness in these acts of deliverance and salvation by which he gathers his people to himself and preserves them.

The word 'justice' is sometimes used in much the same sense and in several passages it appears to be synonymous (Is. 1:27, 5:16, 9:7) with righteousness. But it also comes to mean the requirements which God lays upon his people and indeed is translated as 'law' by RSV in Jeremiah 5:4, 5, 8:7. Yet this is not 'law' in the technical sense of a code of laws but what God requires of those who are his chosen ones, because he has chosen them. Yet again it may refer to the verdict which God pronounces upon men and the punishment which he decrees for those who are disobedient (Jer. 10:24). Because of the depth of Israel's sin this judgement is often very severe (Hosea 5:1, 10:4, Hab. 1:12, Mal. 3:5). His 'justice' then, is God's activity towards his chosen people, good or bad, according to his people's attitude towards him.

The 'steadfast love' of God[97] finds a special place in the teaching of Hosea and Jeremiah. It is extremely difficult to find an entirely satisfactory English equivalent for the Hebrew word often so translated in RSV. In Hosea 2:19 it is placed alongside 'righteousness' and 'justice', but it is a warmer term than either of these. Like them it denotes the activity of God on behalf of his people but doing so in terms of his love and loyalty and his devotion[98] to them (cf. Jer. 9:24, 31:3, 32:18). Sometimes the emphasis is more on the

109

motivation for an action rather than upon the action itself (Joel 2:13).

The fourth characteristic of God is his 'faithfulness' which stresses the firm stability of the purpose of God, the unswerving loyalty and reliability. It is often coupled with 'steadfast love' and the AV translated the pair of words by the phrase 'mercy and truth'.

Yahweh is seen, then, as a God who has chosen Israel as his people and therefore acts towards them in accordance with the demands of that relationship, saving them or punishing them as the case may be. These acts are both motivated by and carried out in love and loyalty and God can be relied upon completely to continue this relationship with his people.

As we might expect the relationship also demands that these qualities should be reciprocated and that man should behave towards God in exactly the same way. Man too must be righteous, and that means not simply obeying a written code of law but behaving as the chosen of God. The law is simply a guide to what God requires and is given to assist men to make the proper response to God. Micah (6:8) thus places justice and steadfast love side by side as the attitudes and actions required by God. Isaiah again and again calls for faithfulness, a steady trust and loyalty towards God. Though the RSV translates this rightly as 'belief' it is nevertheless the same Hebrew root as that which conveys the idea of stability in God himself (Is. 7:9, 28:16, 30:15).

Further, and it is here that the prophets express themselves most clearly and forcibly, the fact that God is righteous, just, loving and stable means that each person within the chosen people must demonstrate those same qualities in his relationships with fellow Israelites. Each Israelite is to treat his brother in the same way as God treats them both, with a due recognition that membership in the chosen people involves responsibilities, the fulfilment of which is righteousness. Justice is the way of life and the more organized system of laws which allows for this fulfilment. That steadfast love is required simply indicates that this is not a matter of keeping an external code of laws or adhering to the will of an arbitrary and despotic God, but is rather an attitude which springs out of the warm recognition of their togetherness as the community, the

110

people of God. It is this aspect of their teaching which gives to the prophetic words their high moral tone. Naturally all this expresses itself often in care for the less fortunate members of Israelite society, the poor and the oppressed, the widow, the orphan and the alien (Is. 10:2, Mic. 2:9, Jer. 5:28, Amos 2:7 etc.). If there is any truth in the claim that Amos is the prophet of righteousness and Hosea the prophet of love it is only that they emphasize different facets of God's nature and activity and of man's required response to him.

So far we have spoken only of the relationship between God and his people in which these qualities find expression between God and man and between man and man. We have quite deliberately avoided speaking of the 'covenant' relationship.[99] This is because the word covenant is usually used to denote a clearly defined and worked out relationship with a definite structure and form and it is by no means certain that this can be found in the prophetic writings. In recent years it has been argued that the form and structure of the covenant is dependent upon certain treaties made by a certain people called Hittites who were prominent and active in the Near East especially between 1500 and 1100 BC. When they captured small states they made with them the so-called suzerainty treaties in which the Hittite overlord gave his name and details of the way in which the subject people had become his vassal. Next the treaty set out a series of commands which would regulate the behaviour of the vassal state and the sanctions to be applied if these commands were not obeyed. It was then argued that such a covenant was made by Yahweh with Israel at Mount Sinai and that the form in which it was understood and described was very similar to that of the Hittite treaties.

The fact that the Hittites were active in this period when the Israelite tribes were leaving Egypt and settling in Canaan and that their treaty forms may have been known as far south as Kadesh where some parts of later Israel spent a considerable time provided some support for the theory. In addition the story of the exodus covenant in Exodus 19–24 was said to follow a similar pattern to the Hittite treaties. Yet one curious feature has always been noticed, namely that the 8th century prophets made no use whatsoever of the term 'covenant'.

111

Various explanations of this have been attempted such as that the term had become so devalued and misunderstood that it was no longer serviceable. Yet it has been assumed that the prophets spoke against the background of the covenant and developed their teaching on the basis of it without actually mentioning it in so many words. The strong condemnations of disobedience which the prophets uttered were thought to be developments of the covenant treaty curses applicable to those who disobeyed the terms of the covenant. There is indeed some similarity between the two, but since curses were common enough outside the context of treaties it cannot really be assumed that the prophets were borrowing treaty forms.

In the same way it was noticed that the prophets used the forms of speech common in the law courts (*see* ch. 7), in which, for instance, they called upon heaven and earth as witnesses, recounted what Yahweh had done for them, uttered the indictment against them and pronounced sentence (Is. 1:2ff.). Since similar forms were found in the suzerainty treaties it was argued that again the prophets were dependent upon them, especially since the covenant was thought to have been renewed at regular intervals and that such a renewal would involve a sort of legal examination of Israel's behaviour. As with the curses, however, it must be remembered that law suits took place every day outside the context of the covenant between Israel and Yahweh and in the context of a dispute between neighbours. These courts must have been familiar enough to the prophets and there is no good reason why their 'law suit' forms should not spring from this normal legal practice in Israel.

It has also been argued that the prophets were the descendants of the 'covenant-spokesman' of the confederacy of Israelite tribes during the days of the Judges.[100] The so-called Minor Judges fulfilled this role and it became an established office. But it is now questioned whether there ever was such a well-organized confederacy of tribes[101] which had special offices of this kind and the link between any supposed covenant-spokesman and the prophets is a tenuous one indeed.

More recently still it has been questioned whether Israel

112

understood her relationship with God in any formal way as a covenant until after the late 8th or 7th century book of Deuteronomy.[102] Certainly the phrase regularly used of the covenant, 'I will be their God and they shall be my people', is not found prior to the 7th century and only in writings which show some dependence on Deuteronomy. Consequently it is no longer safe to assume that the 8th century prophets were aware of or dependent on any formally constructed pattern of covenant relationship upon which they could base their preaching. This is why in chapter 9 no reference was made to covenant traditions. It is safer to speak of election traditions which express the relationship without the more formalized structure of the suzerainty treaties. Election, the choice of Israel by Yahweh as his people, is the supreme expression of God's righteousness, justice, love and stability which by its very nature demands a reciprocal response towards both Yahweh and one's fellow Israelite.

Sin, for the prophets, is simply the failure to make this response and so to recognize one's dependence upon the God who has called Israel into being. Both parts of the chosen people, both Israel and Judah, are deeply guilty of such failure. Some of their sins are directly against Yahweh. Amos speaks of it as 'rebellion' which is a better translation than RSV's 'transgression' (1:3, 6, 9 etc.) while Isaiah, as we have seen, condemns Israel's pride (2:11, 17). Hosea characterizes it as disloyalty (ch. 2) and applies to it the metaphor of harlotry (4:15 etc.) as does Jeremiah (3:1ff.). It may express itself in simple disobedience (Hosea 11) or idolatry (Amos 5:26, Ezek. 8 etc.) or misplaced trust (Is. 7 and Jer. 7) or insincere worship (Is. 1:10ff.).

Other sins are a failure to regard one's fellows as members of the same community to which God has offered himself and to treat them as God has treated Israel. There is robbery (Amos 3:10, Hos. 7:1, Mic. 2:2, Hab. 2:9), violence (Amos 3:10, Is. 5:7, Mic. 3:2, 6:12, Hab. 1:2f., Ezek. 7:11), oppression of the poor (Amos 4:1, Mic. 2:2, Is. 3:14, Zeph. 3:1), dishonest trading (Amos 8:5, Mic. 6:11, Hos. 12:8), luxurious indifference (Amos 6:4ff., Is. 3:6ff., 5:11) adultery (Hos. 7:4), law breaking (Hos. 4:2, 8:1, 8:12), charging interest on loans and mortgages (Is. 5:8, Mic. 7:3), and

113

corruption of the courts (Amos 2:6ff., Is. 1:26, 5:23, 10:1ff., Mic. 3:9, Hab. 1:4, Jer. 5:28). It will readily be seen that many of these expressions of sin correspond to what is forbidden in the Decalogue (Exod. 20:2-17) and it has been argued that this code underlies their condemnations. Certainly Hosea 4:1f. with its reference to swearing, lying, killing, stealing, committing adultery is very close to it. Yet sin is not simply a breach of regulations, whether the Decalogue or some other; it is an act of rebellion against Yahweh himself who has called Israel into being and a failure to be loyal and faithful to him as he has been loyal and faithful to Israel.

17. Judgement, Wrath and Punishment

The prophets shared with the other Old Testament writers the belief that there was an inevitable and inexorable link between behaviour and its consequences. This is expressed most forcibly in the book of Deuteronomy which has strong connections with prophecy. The positive side of the equation is found, for instance, in Deuteronomy 4:40 where Israel is exhorted to keep the commandments of God 'that it may go well with you' (cf. also 5:29, 5:33, 6:2, 6:18, 6:24). The negative finds expression in chapter 6:14ff. where Israel is warned not to go after other gods 'lest the anger of the LORD your God be kindled against you and he destroy you from off the face of the earth' (cf. 7:4, 7:10 etc.). The Wisdom Literature shared the same belief (Prov. 10:3, 10:24, 10:30). Clearly such belief is fundamental to Israelite religion no matter in what form men may express themselves. It is, of course, based upon the understanding of God which we demonstrated in the last chapter, the belief that God is just, and that he does not act capriciously but in a firm and reliable way. Since he has made known his will through priests, prophets and wise men any person or nation which chooses a different path will inevitably go astray and end up in disaster.

Both within the prophetic books and outside them this relationship between sin and punishment can be expressed in two ways. First punishment can be thought of as the automatic outcome of sin. G. Von Rad[103] says, 'there is absolutely nothing in the thought of the Old Testament which by and large corresponds to the separation which we make between sin and penalty'. He calls this a 'synthetic' view of life in which men hold together aspects of life which we separate. To illustrate this he refers to a passage in Numbers 32:23, 'but if you are disobedient you will have sinned (*ḥaṭṭa'ṭem*) against

Yahweh, and you will realize that you will meet with your penalty (*hatta't*)'. In this passage the same Hebrew root expresses the idea of both sin and penalty for sin. Sin, then, once committed, is not exhausted until it has burnt itself out in punishment. H. H. Rowley spoke of this as the 'boomerang' action.[104] To put it differently sin has attached to it a homing device and it always homes in on the person who commits the sin. The prophetic 'therefore' which joins the threat to the diatribe in so many prophetic speeches[105] illustrates this most clearly. Woe to those, says Isaiah, whose main aim in life is self-indulgence. *Therefore* men die and go into exile (Is. 5:11-13). The automatic, causal connection between sin and punishment is thus asserted (cf. Is. 1:19ff., Amos 6:4-6 for further examples).

On the other hand, in Israelite thought nothing happens purely automatically, but every event is due directly to the activity of God. The natural orders of day and night, summer and winter come one after the other regularly, but only because God so promised that they would (Gen. 8:22). Yet it is God himself who brings the sun out each morning and moves it across the sky. Should he wish to make it stand still for an hour or two in order to help Israel in her battles he can do so (Josh. 10:12ff.). The same is true in the moral sphere. The moral order, no matter how automatic it may appear, is always under the direct control of God. This is why the prophets may equally well speak of God punishing a man or a nation in a very personal way. Punishment is a direct act of God. In Isaiah 9:13-17 the removal of all leadership from Israel is not said to be the automatic effect of their failure to turn to God. It is actually God himself who removes them and it is stated in the strongest terms that the Lord has no compassion on the fatherless and widows (cf. Amos 2:13, 5:16f.). There is no way in which these harsh sayings can be made less harsh without doing an injustice to the prophetic way of thinking.

Whichever way it may be expressed the fact that failure to submit to and live by the will of God can only bring disaster demonstrates that sin is a desperately serious matter for both individuals and nations. This is so even though the effect does not in every case follow from the cause. Jeremiah may predict that Jehoiakim's dead body will remain unburied (36:30) yet we are told in 2 Kings 24:6 that he 'slept with his fathers', a phrase which suggests a normal death and burial. We have already seen how Jeremiah himself recognized that it was possible to sin and get away with it (Jer. 12:1). But the strong way in which the relationship between sin and punishment is expressed both indicated and inculcated a very serious view of sin and a strong belief in the justice and reliability of God.

This judging, punishing activity of God is not infrequently referred to as the wrath or anger of God[106] and for the modern reader this often causes difficulty. When the connection between sin and punishment is expressed in automatic terms then we may escape from the difficulty by saying that the wrath of God is simply the automatic out-working of retribution. But the Old Testament writers never hesitate to say that God is angry and in his anger he judges and punishes. We have to come to terms with this and seek to understand it. Naturally enough the words for anger occur frequently in the prophetic books. The one word *'ap*, which literally means the 'nostril' but then comes to mean 'anger' (presumably because anger is expressed by snorting!) occurs no less than fourteen times in Isaiah 1–39, five in Isaiah 40–65, twenty three in Jeremiah, eleven in Ezekiel, four in Hosea, once in Joel, once in Amos, twice each in Micah, Nahum and Habakkuk, three times in Zephaniah and once in Zechariah – and there are other terms for wrath beside this one!

How, then, is this wrath to be related to the love of God? Does God fluctuate between one and the other? It may look like it for certainly his wrath can be 'turned aside' and he can be made to change his mind about the punishment, for instance in response to the prayers of Amos (7:3, 7:6). Yet the wrath of God is never something that merely blows hot and cold; it is always a response to the sin of man. It does not really stand in contradiction to the love of God. Indeed love and anger are not really opposites at all for we rarely get angry over things or with people about whom we do not care deeply. The same is true of the prophetic view about the wrath of God. He is angry with Israel *because* he cares for her and has chosen her. God does not change. Rather if Israel's relationship to him is one of love and obedience then she

117

experiences him as love; but if her attitude is one of rebellion against his will then she experiences the same God as wrath. As J. N. Schofield has put it so well, 'the same wind from God blows one ship to harbour and another on to rocks, in accord with the way the sails of the boats are set'.[107] In the pre-exilic period in particular the prophets believed that the sails were set in such a way that shipwreck was inevitable for Israel and Judah; and it was their fault, not God's, for he had provided them with skilled pilots (the prophets) who sought to persuade them to alter the set of their sails but whom they ignored.

By her sin, then, Israel changes her relationship with God so that he ceases to be a protecting God and becomes a punishing God. By so doing she puts herself in precisely the same relationship as any other nation. So Amos can proclaim the word of God which indicates that Israel is no different from the Ethiopians, the Philistines or the Syrians (9:7). She has forfeited her position as the chosen people of God. So too in Isaiah 28:21 Yahweh comes to fight, as he has done so often in the past; only this time he comes to fight *against* Israel and the prophet describes this work as 'strange' and 'alien'. At his call the message entrusted to Isaiah was one which would in fact harden the people's hearts still further and hasten the judgement, for their sin had already taken them beyond the point of no return. Once God has looked away from Israel (Is. 1:15) she is abandoned to her enemies. Yet this again can be expressed much more sharply by saying that God sends her enemies upon her, raising up the Assyrians to punish her (Is. 10:5f.). When God visits her he does so no longer for good but for evil (Hos. 2:13, Jer. 5:9, 9:9 – where RSV has translated the Hebrew as 'punish'). His eye which has guided his people is now upon them for punishment (Jer. 16:17f., Ezek. 7:4, 7:9).

The punishment which the prophets see as inevitable may or may not be described precisely and clearly. Indeed the form of it matters little; it is the fact of it that is important. Sometimes therefore it is expressed rather vaguely. It is the terror of Yahweh (Is. 2:10) or like the ravaging of a vineyard (Is. 5:5). All cities will be forsaken (Jer. 4:29). It may be famine, wild beasts, pestilence, blood or sword (Ezek. 5:17,

118

14:13ff.). Metaphorically it may be like dry rot or a moth (Hos. 5:12) or like being pressed down under a cart-wheel (Amos 2:13). It may be darkness (Amos 5:18-20) or deprivation of food or joy (Joel 1:15ff.) or driving out women and children from their houses (Mic. 2:9). The language to describe the punishment of God is as rich and varied as this.

Sometimes there is a clear reference to foreign armies though these cannot always be identified with certainty. This is especially true of the earlier prophecies of Jeremiah where he speaks of a 'foe from the north' (6:1) or a 'nation from afar' (5:14ff.). The vagueness here may be due to the fact that it was not clear who were to be the successors of the Assyrians now that their empire was declining. It has sometimes been taken as referring to the Scythians who were making raids on the northern frontiers of Assyria or, alternatively, as meaning divinely sent people, since the north is the mythical home of the gods in Canaanite religion.

But when it became clear to Jeremiah that the Babylonian empire was to succeed the Assyrian then, in his later ministry, the agents of Yahweh's punishment are the Babylonians under Nebuchadnezzar. The earlier prophets, Isaiah and Hosea, both have Assyria clearly in mind (Is. 10:5, Hos. 10:6, 11:5) while Amos mentions no particular people at all.

While God's judgement is usually seen to be upon the nation, Israel or Judah, threats may from time to time be made against individuals within the nation, such as Ahaz (Is. 7:17), Shebna and Eliakim (Is. 22:15ff.), Hezekiah (Is. 38), Jehoiakim (Jer. 36:30), Hananiah the prophet (Jer. 28:15), Passhur the priest (Jer. 20), Amaziah the priest or Jeroboam the king (Amos 7:10ff.).

It may also be directed against foreign nations. It seems to be assumed that although such nations have not had a revelation of God comparable to Israel's there is sufficient revealed to them, presumably by nature, to know that certain actions are wrong and therefore deserve to be punished. Consequently most of the prophetic books have a section which contains oracles against foreign nations. Such a section is found in Amos 1:1–2:3 and the interesting thing here is that the sins for which the nations are condemned are not all sins against Israel but sins one against another. Damascus has 'threshed' Gilead, Moab has burned the bones of the king of Edom. These sins which are against the natural laws of common humanity bring down punishment upon those who perpetrate them. Amongst foreign nations, as in Israel and Judah, pride figures prominently as deserving judgement. Isaiah claims that when Assyria has finished punishing Judah she will regard it purely as a military victory achieved by her own strength of arms and will fail to acknowledge any indebtedness to Yahweh for it (Is. 10:7-19). For this Yahweh will punish Assyria in turn. Jeremiah threatens Moab with the judgement of God because he 'magnified himself against the LORD (48:26). In Ezekiel the prince of Tyre is a kind of second Adam. Just as the first man's pride was his undoing so shall also this prince's (28:1ff.), while Egypt, who thinks she made the Nile, will become a desolation (29:9f.). The whole book of Obadiah is directed against Edom because 'the pride of your heart has deceived you' (v. 3) and the whole book of Nahum against Nineveh, the capital of Assyria who will be brought low because of her attacks on Judah.

This strong connection between sin and punishment therefore operates at all levels and among all peoples. It can, as we shall see, be averted or postponed by repentance and sometimes by sheer grace, but generally sin leads straight to judgement and it is only beyond the judgement that any hope can be offered.

18. Repentance, Faith and Forgiveness

The English word 'repent' is used today almost exclusively in religious contexts and therefore stands in need of explanation in religious terms. The corresponding Hebrew word (*šub*) had no such limitations. It simply meant 'to turn' or 'to return, go back' and could be used in such everyday phrases as 'Go back home!' In religious contexts its meaning was the same. It had nothing immediately to do with weeping or being sorry or making apologies. It involved a 'return', a reorientation of life and behaviour, a change of direction. When applied to men it indicated a 'turning away' from idols or self-reliance and a 'turning towards' God. This being so, it corresponds more closely to the English word 'conversion'.

But the Old Testament can also speak of God 'repenting' (Amos 7:3) and here, of course, it has nothing to do with sin but, as we have noted in the last chapter, indicates the possibility of God doing an 'about turn' in respect of his attitude and activity towards Israel, treating them with favour instead of punishing them as they deserved. However, it is with men as its subject that it is most frequently used. Even here it can be used in the severely practical sense of Israel 'returning' from exile in Babylon or of some other change of fortune. More important for our purpose, though, is the fact that the prophets do sometimes call for that radical change which the word expresses, demanding it from individuals and especially from the chosen people of Israel and Judah. Instead of going through life with their eyes fixed on idols or on themselves, they are urged to turn their gaze upon Yahweh and walk again in the direction he desires for them.

In spite of the insistence among the pre-exilic prophets that God's judgement was inevitable we do find them from time to time calling for repentance and this does appear to be inconsistent for presumably if the call were heeded punishment would be averted, whereas they seem to regard it as inevitable. The tension here cannot simply be removed by attributing the calls to repentance to later users and editors of the prophets' oracles. It seems rather that the pre-exilic prophets regarded the door of hope as closed and barred from man's side. They could see no prospect of the repentance which would unlock the door and make rescue possible. On the other hand their understanding of God was such that they had to leave room for the possibility that God could withdraw his punishment and therefore on those grounds they had to appeal for repentance. The appeal must be made because it was consistent with their understanding of God but they knew it was useless because Israel had passed beyond the point where she could change direction. Her sin would have to be dealt with not so much by the forgiveness which is God's response to repentance, but by the cleansing and refining of judgement.

Apart from its final chapter the book of Amos sees no hope whatever for Israel and there is much to suggest that the final verses of hope in 9:9b-15 were not originally those of Amos but were a conclusion reached by the editors who were using Amos' preaching in the Southern Kingdom of Judah. Yet in 5:4, 'Seek me and live; but do not seek Bethel', there is a clear call to the kind of repentance outlined above and in 5:15 it 'may be' that the LORD will be gracious at least to the remnant of Joseph. The cult of Bethel has been the driving force for the life of Israel and since this was syncretistic and debased it could lead only to destruction. They must allow Yahweh once again to be their driving force. But that Amos saw this to be impossible is shown by the very next verse or two in which the future is completely and utterly dark (5:18-20).

In the same way Micah sees that it would be possible for Judah to escape the punishment of Yahweh if only the people would turn their backs upon mere reliance on multitudes of sacrifices and look again to those qualities of life which characterize God himself – justice, devotion and humility (6:8). That such a change is seen to be impossible is shown by the fact that he is certain that 'Zion shall be ploughed as a field; Jerusalem shall become a heap of ruins' (3:12).

In the northern prophet Hosea the possibility of repentance seems to be expressed more emphatically. The quotation of the people's decision to return to the LORD (6:1) is not merely an ironic repetition of the people's insincere words. Hosea seems to hope that this is what they will say and do. This repentance is accompanied by a confession of guilt (5:15) and if NEB is correct in translating the first verb in 6:3 as 'let us humble ourselves' then it is from this position of confession and humility that they may 'press on to know Yahweh'. But for all this the real door of hope, even for Hosea, lies beyond the impending punishment when Israel will be given a fresh opportunity to show her obedience and loyalty (2:15).

As we have seen the call of Isaiah leaves no room at all for repentance, yet even he can see the possibility of it. The well known verses in 1:18-20 may be translated in a number of different ways. 'If your sins are like scarlet, shall they be white as snow?' which implies a negative answer and rules out the possibility of forgiveness altogether; 'Though your sins are like scarlet they shall be white as snow' (RSV), which seems to make forgiveness unconditional; 'Though your sins are like scarlet, they may become white as snow' (NEB), which makes forgiveness conditional and leaves open the possibility that if they become 'willing and obedient' God will spare them.

Again, in the name of Isaiah's first son (7:3), Shear-jashub, there may be a promise that at least a few people, a remnant, will repent and the future will open up through them. Here, however, the context of the confrontation with Ahaz seems to demand a threat rather than a promise and the name can be interpreted as meaning that only those few people who happen to escape the judgement when it comes will, having seen it, repent and return to God whereas for the vast majority there is no escape from destruction. The name is thus ambivalent and is perhaps intended to be so.

Finally the possibility of forgiveness is repeated at 30:15 only to be followed at once by 'but ye would not'. The matter is further complicated in Isaiah by the fact that Hezekiah apparently did repent and begin some religious reforms

(36:7, cf. 2 Kings 19) and the destruction of Jerusalem did not take place until a century later. All Judah was devastated except the capital (1:8) and Isaiah in fact promised that the Assyrians would not shoot an arrow into it (37:33). The harsh message of certain judgement, total in its effect upon Judah, was modified at least to the extent that the destruction of Jerusalem was postponed for a hundred years.

By then Jeremiah felt himself caught on the horns of a dilemma. He is confident that Jerusalem and Judah must fall to the Babylonians, but again the book pleads for repentance and amendment of life. Jeremiah 6:16 is not unlike Isaiah 30:15 in its call to return to the way of life of past days when the people were faithful. The appeal however fell upon deaf ears, as it was bound to: 'We will not give heed.' The situation in 7:1-20 is more complicated. Apart from verses 3, 5-7, the chapter is one of unconditional destruction and Jeremiah is even forbidden to pray for his people (v. 16). Yet those four verses do introduce the possibility of amendment of life. Now there is little doubt that the book of Jeremiah attained its present form through the work of the Deuteronomists[108] and there is every likelihood that these verses express their views, rather than the views of Jeremiah himself. Finally in chapter 14 the Judaeans appear to acknowledge their guilt, but either they are insincere or it is too late, for Yahweh will not listen and again Jeremiah is forbidden to pray.

So no way of return now remains open except through the fires of judgement in destruction and exile. It is no accident, therefore, that in Isaiah 40–55 the question of repentance and return to Yahweh is not raised. Judah had passed the point of no return and her sins could only be dealt with by punishment. But now, by the exile, they have been so dealt with. 'Her iniquity is pardoned, she has received from the LORD's hand double for all her sins' (40:2). The future to which this prophet now looks forward is made possible not by the people's repentance, but by God's new start with this broken and dispirited people.

Later still, in the times of Haggai and Zechariah, the need arose once more to call the people back to a more complete allegiance to Yahweh, symbolized in the rebuilding of the temple. The call to repent (Zech. 1:2) is answered by the people and so Yahweh returns to them. The possibility of repentance is now there because the exile and the return are behind them. In this new era, though people may again sinfully turn away from God, they may also turn back to him.

Little more can be said about faith than has already been said in chapters 9 and 16. It is prominent mainly in the teaching of Isaiah as a call to the kings Ahaz and Hezekiah, and an unsuccessful call at that, to rely wholly on the God who has made his promises to David and through David to Judah. This is not faith in the New Testament sense, of course, but it moves towards it in that it is total reliance on the personal God of Israel to the exclusion of everything else – self, allies or idols.

The prophets, especially those before the exile, are hard men with a hard message. Yet here and there one catches a glimpse of the tensions in which they live. Even an Amos may intercede for the people of Israel, asking for their forgiveness and indeed receiving a positive answer to his prayers after his first two visions (7:3, 7:6). But there came a time when such prayers were no longer to be offered (Jer. 7:16, 14:11). Most, if not all of them, see something of the love of God as well as his wrath expressed not in forgiveness, but in punishment and judgement which opens the door of hope and makes the renewal so brilliantly described by the exilic prophet of Isaiah 40–55 possible for the chosen people whom God has now chosen again.

19. Hopes for the Future

There is little more to be said about the nature of the prophets' hopes for the future than has been said in the course of the preceding chapters, but it will be convenient to draw all this together now and then make some further comments about them.

For the pre-exilic prophets this future always lay on the far side of the judgement of God upon Israel and Judah when they believed God would start all over again with Israel, understood now as referring to the whole people of God and not merely to the Northern Kingdom which came to an end in 722 BC. The way in which that future was envisaged depended upon the traditions of Israel's past with which the prophet was familiar. Hosea saw it as a return to the wilderness (2:15f.) where God would 'allure' her again and make her once more his people. The book of Amos in its present form sees it as a renewal of the Davidic dynasty which will be accompanied by fertility and material prosperity, accompanied by a promise that this will now be permanent (9:9b-15). Isaiah also takes up the idea of a new David, anticipating a son of Jesse whose perfectly just and righteous rule will bring prosperity not only to Israel but to the whole earth and will bring peace and well-being to all creatures as to all men (11:1-9). This new king will bear the throne names of 'Wonderful Counsellor, Mighty God (or god-like hero), Everlasting Father, Prince of Peace' (9:6) and his rule will be unending. The book of Micah, too, looks for a new ruler from Bethlehem, as David was from Bethlehem, who will lead his people into security and raise them up above all other nations (5:2-15). Both Micah (4:1-4) and Isaiah (2:2-4) share an oracle which see a universal acknowledgement of Yahweh as the true God. Zion stands at the centre of the stage and all nations will come there because they will know that the true law which should govern them goes out from his temple there.

126

The future for Jeremiah entails a new covenant made by God with his people, different from the old Mosaic covenant in that Israel's will will conform to Yahweh's will and so the relationship will not be dependent upon the people's ability to obey. This does not make them mere automatons; the relationship will be as close as that between two people who find themselves constantly desiring the same things so that there is no conflict of interests between them (Jer. 31:31ff.). Just occasionally he too can look forward to a new David (30:9) or to a Branch from David (23:5) with Zion restored (30:18, 31:12). Again this new age will be characterized by prosperity (31:12ff.). It belongs not to Israel alone nor to Judah alone but to both nations who together make up the ideal people of God (31:31).

This is true also for Ezekiel who is told to take two sticks, one representing Israel and the other Judah, and join them together. So the total people of God will be restored under one king and become one nation, living as the covenant people again (Ezek. 37:15-28). This will involve a new creation of his people. The dry bones will be gathered together, shaped into a new body by God who will breathe into them once again. In other words, the traditions about the creation of man in Genesis 2:7 are used to describe how God will start again with his people by recreating them (Ezek. 37:1-14). In the long parable of chapter 16 he describes how Israel has consistently spurned all the love which God has showered upon her, yet still he will forgive and establish a new covenant with her (16:60ff.). This, as for Jeremiah, will require a new spirit and a new will in Israel which God will provide after purifying them (36:24-31). So, like a good shepherd, a term which always conjures up the idea of a king as well, he will restore his people gathering them from far and wide and providing them with a new under-shepherd, a Davidic king, to rule over them (ch. 34).

Nahum's view of the future is rather less profound. He is simply concerned with the downfall of the Assyrians and the consequent freedom and exaltation of Judah. In a similar vein Obadiah looks forward to the downfall of Edom and to a time when Mount Zion, the Jews, will rule over Mount Esau, the Edomites, and when all the exile of Judah will be restored to take possession of all the countries surrounding Israel.

With Isaiah 40–55 we return to more far-reaching views based upon past traditions. In the imminent return from Babylon to the homeland of the Jews God will perform a new thing which will form the basis of the new community as surely as the exodus from Egypt formed the basis for the old (43:18f.). The return will thus be nothing less than a second exodus, a new act of redemption brought about by God (41:14). A new wilderness will have to be crossed (40:3-5) but God will smooth out the difficulties for them and indeed the wilderness itself will become fertile (41:19f.). A new 'sea' will be crossed (50:2, 51:10f.). Zion will be comforted (51:3) and the 'ransomed of the LORD' will return there (51:11). It will become again the holy place (52:1) where Yahweh, the divine king, is worshipped (52:7). The future appears to include the figure of the Servant of Yahweh which may be thought of as a royal figure or as a prophetic, Mosaic figure or, perhaps even more likely, as a new figure who combines within himself royal, prophetic and priestly traits.[109]

The post-exilic prophets, Haggai and Zechariah, lived in a day when some of these hopes were fulfilled. Some, at least, of the Jews had returned and re-settled in Judah. The new temple had not yet been built, but the two prophets encouraged the people to work on it. When they showed some disappointment that the temple they were building was not as fine as that of Solomon then Haggai pointed to a day still in the future when all the nations of the earth would bring their treasures to beautify it (2:6-9). It appears that they thought the hopes of a Davidic ruler were already fulfilled in Zerubbabel the governor (Hagg. 2:20, Zech. 3:7-10, 4:6-10), but Zerubbabel now disappears from the scene for reasons which we can no longer know.[110] With him also disappear all immediate hopes of a Jewish king and from now on Judah is governed by priests.

The truth is that although the Jews were permitted to return to their own land by the Persian emperor, Cyrus, in 538 BC and although from then on they continued their new existence there as the people of God, very many of those hopes which had been expressed by the prophets remained unfulfilled.

128

There is no sign of the people deported from the Northern Kingdom in 722 BC returning as Hosea imagined and therefore no sign of a united kingdom of north and south, Israel and Judah, as Jeremiah and Ezekiel had hoped for. No new David, nor even a son of David arose to govern the people in righteousness and the kind of prosperity associated with his reign never materialized. Indeed the Jews who did return in 538 BC seem to have had a struggle to maintain themselves in Judah.

Zion, it is true, was rebuilt as a walled city by Nehemiah and once again it had its temple, but as for being exalted as the chief city in the world nothing could be further from the truth. The great nations which surrounded Judah over the next few centuries were in a position, if they so wished, to ignore Jerusalem and certainly did not flow to it to hear the Law of God so that they may become adherents and find the true way of life through him. In fact by the 2nd century BC the Jews were having a real struggle to uphold their faith against considerable Greek influence. No suffering servant of God arose, either priestly or prophetic, to enable Israel to shine like a light in the gentile world and draw other peoples to her God. Were these hopes then mere pipe dreams of men who were unable to face the reality of the situation? We could say so if their predictions had been based simply on their own wishful thinking. In fact they were founded upon the prophets' belief in God whose love for his people continues through thick and thin and who cannot simply leave them cast off for ever.

Either their view of God had been completely mistaken or else their hopes and God's promises to them had to remain in force awaiting fulfilment in the days that still lay ahead. These hopes and promises therefore became a feature of Judaism, and Jews have continued to wait for their Messiah, their anointed one, who would establish a new Jewish kingdom on earth.

Christian people have dealt with these hopes differently. Just as the old traditions of Israel needed to be re-interpreted so also these hopes were re-interpreted by the early Christians so that Jesus Christ was seen as the fulfilment of the hopes of a new David and of the Suffering Servant. The universal kingdom was seen not as a kingdom in the earthly, political sense

129

but as the rule of God in the hearts and lives of men. The Christian church was the new Israel through whom the promises of God were to reach the world. She was to be a light to the Gentiles until all nations were drawn through Christ to God the Father. It was in this sense that the New Testament could then take up the prophetic predictions of the Old Testament and apply them to Christ and it is legitimate for us to do the same. We must not say therefore that the prophets predicted the coming of Jesus; we can say that their hopes for the future stand in need of this radical re-interpretation in the light of the coming of Jesus and so remain relevant for his followers.

Even so, for the Christian church there still remains a hope beyond the fulfilment in Christ. We may still look for his coming again and for the establishment of his kingdom in all its fullness. We may still think of the new Jerusalem that lies somewhere in the future when his rule is acknowledged by all men and there is universal peace. The hopes of the prophets are not yet exhausted, but flow into the Christian hope and enrich it. So by their hope and confidence in God these great figures of Israel's past may help us to grasp more fully the meaning of the coming of Christ and to maintain our hope for the future and our faith in the promises of God.

Notes

1. *Oxford Advanced Learners Dictionary of Current English*, p. 682.
2. J. Lindblom, *Prophecy in Ancient Israel*, Oxford, 1973, p. 1.
3. Many now place the J strand or some other 'ground work' in the reign of Solomon. Cf., for instance, G. Fohrer, *Introduction to the Old Testament*, London, 1970, p. 130, O. Kaiser, *Introduction to the Old Testament*, E. Tr., Oxford, 1975, pp. 82f. and also G. Von Rad, *Old Testament Theology*, Edinburgh and London, 1965, vol. II, pp. 3f.
4. Op. cit., pp. 29–46.
5. Op. cit., pp. 1–6.
6. The texts are reproduced in translation with some discussion in M. Noth, 'History and the Word of God', in *The Laws in the Pentateuch, and other Essays*, E. Tr., Edinburgh and London, 1966.
7. The word translated 'men of the south' is exactly equivalent to the Old Testament name 'benjamin' which literally means 'son of the right hand', the 'right hand' being the south when facing eastwards.
8. It may be read in full in translation in W. K. Simpson (ed.), *The Literature of Ancient Egypt*, New Haven and London, 1973, pp. 142–155.
9. W. K. Simpson, op. cit., pp. 234–240.
10. Op. cit., p. 6.
11. Op. cit., pp. 7f.
12. *Theology of the Old Testament*, E. Tr., London, 1960, vol. I, pp. 309ff.
13. Op. cit., p. 66.
14. G. Von Rad, op. cit., p. 7, n. 1.
15. T. C. Vriezen, *The Religion of Ancient Israel*, E. Tr., London, 1967, pp. 206f.

16. Op. cit., pp. 298ff.
17. Op. cit., pp. 4f.
18. Op. cit., pp. 101ff.
19. Op. cit., pp. 8f.
20. Op. cit., pp. 1–6.
21. In chapter 10, pp. 67–71.
22. E. W. Nicholson, *Preaching to the Exiles*, Oxford, 1971.
23. Cf. G. A. Smith, *The Book of Isaiah*, revd. ed., London, 1927, W. Eichrodt, op. cit., vol. II, p. 432, but cf. also O. Kaiser, *Isaiah 1–12*. E. Tr., London, 1972, pp. 82f.
24. J. Lindblom, op. cit., p. 187, G. Von Rad, op. cit., p. 151.
25. J. Lindblom, op. cit., p. 134.
26. H. W. Wolff, *Anthropology of the Old Testament*, E. Tr., London, 1974, p. 8 calls this 'synthetic' thinking.
27. See chapter 8.
28. Cf. Von Rad, op. cit., pp. 80ff.
29. Von Rad, op. cit., pp. 36ff., J. Lindblom, op. cit., pp. 103f., C. Westerman, *Basic Forms of Prophetic Speech*, E. Tr., London, 1967, pp. 98ff.
30. G. Von Rad, op. cit., pp. 73ff., C. Westerman, op. cit., pp. 169ff.
31. 'Symbolic action' in J. Lindblom, op. cit., pp. 165ff., G. Von Rad, op. cit., pp. 95ff.
32. W. O. E. Oesterley and T. H. Robinson, *Hebrew Religion*, London, 1930, pp. 75ff.
33. See above, p. 25.
34. Cf. W. Eichrodt, *Ezekiel*, London, 1970, pp. 75f., W. Wevers, *Ezekiel*, London, 1969, p. 58.
35. G. A. Cooke, *Ezekiel*, Edinburgh, 1936, pp. 47f.
36. W. Eichrodt, *Ezekiel*, E. Tr., London, 1970, pp. 75f.
37. W. O. E. Oesterley and T. H. Robinson, op. cit., p. 241, J. Lindblom, op. cit., pp. 187ff., G. Von Rad, op. cit., pp. 21f., but cf., pp. 165ff.
38. E. W. Nicholson, op. cit., R. E. Clements, *Prophecy and Tradition*, Oxford, 1975, pp. 41f.
39. R. E. Clements, op. cit., p. 51.
40. See H. H. Rowley, 'The Marriage of Hosea' in *Men of God*, London, 1963, pp. 66–97 for a full discussion of the problem. Cf. also G. Von Rad, op. cit., pp. 140ff.

41. J. Bright, *History of Israel*, 2nd ed., London, 1972, M. Noth, *History of Israel*, E. Tr., London, 1958, S. Herrmann, *A History of Israel in Old Testament Times*, E. Tr., London, 1975.

42. The dates of the various kings of Israel and Judah are uncertain and are differently given in various histories. The problem is a difficult and complex one, but does not concern us here.

43. The most common view is that the book was either all or part of the book of Deuteronomy. Many now think the book originated in the north. For the present author's view see H. Mowvley, *The Testimony of Israel*, Oxford, 1971, pp. 24f.

44. See above, pp. 32f.

45. The literary problems underlying Zech. 9:9-14 are complex. For a full discussion see P. R. Ackroyd, *Exile and Restoration*, London, 1968, pp. 194ff.

46. See chapter 19.

47. For a discussion of the location of this see O. Kaiser, *Isaiah 1–12*, London, 1972, pp. 89ff.

48. For the contention that much biblical material, and especially the book of Job, is properly to be described as poetry see A. Quiller-Couch, *On the Art of Reading*, Cambridge, 1920, pp. 130ff.

49. G. Von Rad, op. cit., vol. I, pp. 109f.

50. For a fuller discussion of the metrical structure of Hebrew poetry see O. Eissfeldt, *The Old Testament: an Introduction*, E. Tr., Oxford, 1966, pp. 57ff.

51. Op. cit., vol. II, p. 38 n. 9.

52. Von Rad, op. cit., pp. 72ff. Cf. O. Kaiser, *Introduction to the Old Testament*, E. Tr., Oxford, 1975, p. 293.

53. G. Von Rad, op. cit., vol. II, pp. 3ff.

54. R. E. Clements, op. cit., pp. 2f.

55. So W. Eichrodt, *Theology of the Old Testament*, vol. II, London, 1967, p. 328, G. Von Rad, op. cit., vol. II, pp. 212ff. Some scholars have taken the view that the new covenant differs from the old in the fact that the law is internalized. Cf. J. Skinner, *Prophecy and Religion*, Cambridge, 1926, p. 329.

56. W. Eichrodt, op. cit., vol. I, p. 483 n. 4.

57. G. Von Rad, op. cit., vol. II, pp. 258ff.
58. Because this prophet is able to combine many traditional pictures it seems wiser to regard the Servant as a future figure who is described with the help not of one tradition, kingly *or* prophetic, but of a combination of both.
59. G. Von Rad, op. cit., vol. II, p. 123, Eichrodt, op. cit., vol. I, pp. 459ff.
60. S. Mowinkel, *He That Cometh*, E. Tr., Oxford, 1956, pp. 132f., and *The Psalms in Israel's Worship*, E. Tr., Oxford, 1962, pp. 116f.
61. G. Von Rad, op. cit., vol. II, p. 136.
62. See above, p. 53.
63. The creation narrative in Gen. 1:1-2, 4a is a later account of creation from the priestly writer in the exilic period. This narrative was thus not available to the pre-exilic prophets, though of course the tradition underlying it may have been. The earlier tradition in Gen. 2.4bff. was certainly known and available in written form.
64. So N. H. Snaith, *The Jewish New Year Festival*, London, 1947, pp. 36f., 200ff.
65. R. E. Clements, op. cit., p. 46. The whole of Clements' chapter 4, 'The Role of the Prophet according to Israelite Tradition', is a very important contribution to the questions under discussion here.
66. Cf. H. H. Rowley, 'Was Amos a Nabi'?', in *Festschrift O. Eissfeldt*, Halle, 1947, pp. 194ff., J. L. Mays, *Amos*, London, 1969, pp. 137ff.
67. J. Lindblom, op. cit., pp. 161f., 367ff.
68. Ibid.
69. Ibid.
70. Ibid.
71. J. Lindblom, op. cit., pp. 225ff.
72. Not all commentators on Amos take this view. Von Rad (op. cit., p. 138) regards these verses as a genuine saying of Amos.
73. G. Von Rad, op. cit., vol. I, p. 221.
74. E. W. Nicholson, *Deuteronomy and Tradition*, Oxford, 1967, pp. 65ff.

75. M. Noth, *History of Israel*, pp. 42ff.
76. Cf. especially with regard to Jeremiah. E. W. Nicholson, *Preaching to the Exiles*, Oxford, 1971, and R. E. Clements, op. cit., pp. 46ff.
77. *Against Apion*, 1.8.
78. For alternative views see many of the standard *Introductions*. e.g. O. Eissfeldt, op. cit., pp. 306ff.
79. E. J. Young, *Studies in Isaiah*, Grand Rapids, 1954 takes the opposite view that the whole of our book of Isaiah comes from the 8th century Isaiah of Jerusalem. Cf. R. K. Harrison, *Introduction to the Old Testament*, London, 1970, pp. 764ff.
80. H. H. Rowley, 'The Prophets and Sacrifice' in *Expository Times*, 58 (1946–7), pp. 305–307, and *The Unity of the Bible*, London, 1953, pp. 30ff.
81. M. Noth, *A History of Pentateuchal Traditions*, E. Tr., New Jersey, 1972, pp. 59ff., G. Von Rad, op. cit., vol. I, pp. 187ff.
82. See especially A. R. Johnson, *The Cultic Prophet in Ancient Israel*, Cardiff, 1962.
83. H. H. Rowley, *Worship in Ancient Israel*, London, 1967, pp. 165f.
84. G. Henton Davies, 'Psalm 95' in *Zeitschrift für alttestamentliche Wissenschaft*, 83, 1973, pp. 183–95.
85. J. H. Eaton, *Psalms*, London, 1967, p. 232.
86. For excellent discussions of the Wisdom Literature see G. Von Rad, *Wisdom in Israel*, E. Tr., London, 1972 (a fuller treatment than in his *Old Testament Theology*, vol. I, pp. 418–459), W. McKane, *Prophets and Wise Men*, London, 1965, R. E. Clements, *Prophecy and Tradition*, Oxford, 1975, pp. 73–83.
87. H. H. Rowley, *The Relevance of Apocalyptic*, London, 1944.
88. E. H. Heaton, *Daniel*, London, 1956.
89. For a discussion of the nature of apocalyptic see N. W. Porteous, *Daniel*, London, 1965, pp. 14ff.
90. Op. cit., p. 17.
91. H. H. Rowley, op. cit., p. 13.
92. See above, p. 67.
93. H. H. Rowley, op. cit., pp. 28ff., W. Eichrodt, op. cit.,

vol. II, pp. 199, 514, G. Von Rad, *Old Testament Theology*, vol. II, Edinburgh and London, 1965, p. 312, Morna D. Hooker, *The Son of Man in Mark*, London, 1967, pp. 1–74.

94. Cf. W. Eichrodt, op. cit., vol. I, pp. 270ff., E. Jacob, *Theology of the Old Testament*, E. Tr., London. 1955, pp. 86ff. for a general discussion of the term 'holiness'.

95. Cf. the discussion of these verses in P. R. Ackroyd, *Exile and Restoration*, London, 1968, pp. 166ff.

96. Cf., among others, J. N. Schofield, *An Introduction to Old Testament Theology*, London, 1964, pp. 41f., G. Von Rad, op. cit., vol. I, pp. 370ff., W. Eichrodt, op. cit., vol. I, pp. 239ff., E. Jacob, op. cit., pp. 103ff.

97. N. Glueck, *Ḥesed in the Bible*, E. Tr., Los Angeles, 1967, W. Eichrodt, op. cit., vol. I, pp. 232ff., E. Jacob, op. cit., pp. 103ff.

98. A. R. Johnson says that this is the nearest English equivalent (*Ḥesed and Ḥasid*) in 'Interpretationes ad VT Sigmund Mowinckel Septuagenario missae, 1955', in *Norsk Teologisk Tidsskrift*, Oslo, 1955, pp. 110:12.

99. Cf. D. H. McCarthy, *Old Testament Covenant*, Oxford, 1972 (where all the relevant literature is listed). Also R. E. Clements, *Prophecy and Tradition*, Oxford, 1975, pp. 8ff.

100. A. Alt, 'The Origins of Israelite Law' in *Essays on Old Testament History and Religion*, E. Tr., Oxford, 1966, pp. 102f., R. E. Clements, op. cit., pp. 9ff.

101. S. Herrmann, *A History of Israel in Old Testament Times*, London, 1975, pp. 112ff., A. D. G. Mayes, 'Israel in the Pre-monarchy period' in *Vetus Testamentum*, 22 (1973), pp. 151–170.

102. D. J. McCarthy, *Treaty and Covenant*, Rome, 1963.

103. Op. cit., vol. I, p. 266.

104. Cf. *The Faith of Israel*, London, 1956, p. 90.

105. See above, p. 48.

106. W. Eichrodt, op. cit., vol. I, pp. 258ff., E. Jacob, op. cit., pp. 114ff.

107. Op. cit., p. 53.

108. See above p. 17. E. W. Nicholson, *Preaching to the Exiles*, Oxford, 1971, especially pp. 116ff.

109. See above, p. 55.
110. It is often thought that he was removed from office by the Persians on account of the messianic hopes which had been placed upon him by the Jews. While this is possible there is no certain evidence to show that it was so. Cf. P. R. Ackroyd, *Exile and Restoration*, London, 1968, p. 147.

Index of Authors

Index of Subjects

141

142

omen, 6
oral (tradition), 4, 44, 63f, 96

palace, 6
parable, 15, 127
parallelism, 45, 77
Passhur, 33, 119
Passover, 79
peace, 56, 126
pentateuch, 49f, 79
people of God, 21, 26, 32, 37, 49ff, 54, 58f, 75, 81, 92, 109ff, 118, 121,
    125, 126ff
Persian, 41, 58, 98, 100, 128
Philistines, 39, 50, 118
Phoenicia, 6
poetry, 44f, 78, 133n
polytheism, 49, 75
power (of God), 19f, 23ff, 43, 105
prayer, 6, 80, 117, 124, 125
prediction, 96, 99, 116, 129f
presence (of God), 53
pride, 105, 108, 113, 120
priest, 7, 11, 33, 46, 84ff, 87, 92, 94, 105f, 115, 128f
Priest, High, 42
professional prophet, 18, 87
promise, 12, 46, 63, 70, 86, 116, 123, 126, 129f
Promised Land, 55, 92
prophetess, 83
prophetic action, 28ff, 43
prophets, classical, 4, 14, 37, 60, 82ff, 94
prostitution (cultic), 76, 84
proverb, 89, 93
providence, 23
psalms, 46, 55, 58, 69, 85f
punish(ment), 21, 30, 38, 41, 47, 50, 54, 69, 99, 104, 109, 110, 115ff,
    121ff

Rahab, 59
redeem(er), 54, 105f
redemption, 54, 128
Red Sea, 54, 57, 59
reform, 21, 123
remnant, 31f, 122f
repentance, 21, 78, 97, 120, 121ff
responsibility, 22, 50, 51
restoration, 41, 46, 53f
revelation, 5, 119
riddle, 93

righteousness, 46, 53, 78, 80f, 107, 108, 113, 126, 129
ro'eh, 10, 12

sacrifice, 6, 11, 77f, 83, 97, 107, 122
salvation, 56, 109f
Samaria, 37, 39, 43, 52, 54, 84
Samson, 24
Samuel, 10, 24
sanctuary, 6, 11f, 46, 54, 79, 82, 87, 106
Saul, 10, 12, 24, 37, 82
school (Deuteronomic), 65f
school – Isaiah, 70; – Wisdom, 89, 92f
scribe, 62
Scythians, 119
sea, 58, 128
seer, 10ff, 87
Seleucid, 98
Servant of the Lord, 24, 34, 55, 128f, 134n
Shaphan, 33
Shear-jashub, 61, 123
Shebna, 119
shepherd, 26, 52, 54, 126
Shiloh, 53
shrine, 78
sin, 19, 31, 51, 54, 56, 68, 76ff, 91, 104, 108f, 113f, 115ff, 121f, 124
Sinai, 79, 111
singers, 87
Solomon, 85f, 90, 96, 128, 131n
Son of God, 52, 86
Son of Man, 99f
sons of prophets, 60
songs – mocking, 46; – wedding, 45f
spirit, 11ff, 14, 24ff, 82, 109, 127
steadfast love, 86, 109f
symbol, 28, 98, 100
symbolism, 96
symbolic action, 15, 28
syncretism, 75, 97, 122
Syria, 26, 29, 39f, 50, 69, 87, 118

Tabernacles, Feast of, 107
Tekoa, 17, 60, 93
temple, 6, 18f, 33, 40ff, 53f, 62f, 65, 68, 76f, 82ff, 87, 97, 106f, 124, 126, 128f
theophany, 85
threat, 4, 48, 68f, 116, 123
Tiglath Pileser, 38f
tradition, 4, 12, 14, 33, 49ff, 64f, 79, 90, 92f, 95f, 98, 100, 113, 126ff, 134n

Index of Biblical References

Old Testament

148

150